CARIBBEAN WRITERS SERIES

36

Caribbean plays for playing

Caribbean plays
for playing

Edited by Keith Noel

HEINEMANN
LONDON · KINGSTON

Heinemann Educational Books Ltd
22 Bedford Square, London WC1B 3HH
PO Box 1028, Kingston, Jamaica

IBADAN   NAIROBI
EDINBURGH   MELBOURNE   AUCKLAND
SINGAPORE   HONG KONG   KUALA LUMPUR   NEW DELHI

Heinemann Educational Books Inc.
70 Court Street, Portsmouth, New Hampshire 03801, USA

© Dennis Scott, Zeno Obi Constance, Aldwyn Bully, Kendel
Hippolyte.
© Notes and Introduction Keith Noel, 1985

British Library Cataloguing in Publication Data

Caribbean plays for playing.—(Caribbean writers
  series; 36)
  1. West Indian drama (English)
  I. Noel, Keith   II. Series
  812′.008′091821   PR9217

  ISBN 0-435-98647-3

Set in 10/11pt Baskerville by Activity Ltd, Salisbury, Wilts
Printed by Richard Clay (The Chaucer Press) Ltd, Bungay,
Suffolk

Contents

To my parents — who opened my eyes.
And Winston, Sharon, Seymour, Ann-Marie, Noel and
the rest of that beautiful bunch — for making me see.

Part I: Introduction

1 *The Commonwealth Caribbean:* the social background

Caribbean society is unique in that it is a migrant society in which the vast majority of its people are descendants of Africans who were brought here against their will to work as slaves on plantations. The next largest ethnic group in the region are the descendants of those (East Indians) who came to work as indentured labourers on these same plantations after the abolition of slavery. During this period of slavery and then indentureship the territories were colonies of various European countries and political and economic power lay in the hands of a minority of people who had come from Europe.

By the late nineteenth century the local planters, some of whom had been born and raised in the Caribbean and who had begun to develop a life-style that was unique to them, had begun to share some of this power.

The church had been involved in educating the descendants of the slaves and indentured labourers and by the end of the first quarter of this century these persons were able to be employed in positions of some prestige.

The 1930s

The 1930s saw the beginning of the final stages in the evolution of a complete way of life that was peculiarly and particularly 'Caribbean'. One significant feature of these Caribbean societies was that they were made up of two (and in some cases three) distinct cultural and social groups, both of which had to look elsewhere for their cultural origins. On the one hand there

1

were the black descendants of the slaves and indentured labourers, who formed the bulk of the population of the society. On the other, there were the white descendants of slave-owners and plantation-owners, who were at the apex of the power structure. They had the businesses, sat in the Legislative Council, were the priests of the established churches, and so on.

Between these two groups were the educated blacks and the mulattoes. Their education was European and was such as to make them lose contact with the rest of their group. It changed their values, their life-style and their outlook on life generally.

A look at the ways in which these sub-cultures entertained themselves is informative. In the performing arts, for example, the black majority indulged themselves in various aspects of folk culture (Cannes Brulles and John Canoe are examples), while the white minority in most cases maintained their taste for things European.

Quite often good amateur productions of the European classics were staged by local groups. This was augmented, in the larger islands, by occasional visits from touring professional groups. Ballet classes were also held and performances given, and recitals of classical European music by foreign and locally trained artistes were not infrequent.

Among the 'middle' group, that of mulattoes and educated blacks, were some who totally rejected the folk forms. But many found that they could move, even if sometimes uneasily, and nearly always self-consciously, between the two cultures. The 1930s and 1940s saw the emergence of writers like C. L. R. James, Claude McKay and Edgar Mittelholzer at the same time as the political fathers of our countries were beginning to struggle to wrest power from Europe. It is not insignificant that many of the new political giants belonged to this middle group – educated enough to battle the holders of power on their own ground, but feeling the throb of the blood of the peasants of the fields in their veins. Norman Manley, Albert Gomes, Albert Marryshow and Grantley Adams are among this group.

The 1940s to the 1960s

Even though the 1930s marked the beginning of a new era in the history of the Commonwealth Caribbean, it was not until the 1960s that this crystallized into political independence. In the years intervening, the sub-cultures that made up the population of the region nervously settled down to coexist and intermix. There developed a social–ethnic continuum out of the three groups. Broadening of educational opportunities led to the growth of a much larger (lower and upper) middle class while intermarriage made the colour continuum much more subtle. At opposite ends of this social/colour continuum were still the two major cultural groups – coming from fundamentally different origins.

The history of the development of Caribbean culture and society from its birth in the 1930s to its adolescence in the 1960s is largely a history of the relationships between these three groups, and the tensions involved in these relationships. The tension between the two groups which existed at opposite ends of this continuum had reverberations in all areas of life. The teacher–student relationship, for example, was often one in which the teacher tried to inculcate the values of the socially powerful 'upper' cultural group into the student, who most often came from the subordinate group. The employer–employee (and consequently the trade union–management) relationship often had the same socio-ethnic factor involved. Policemen, too, were often seen as protecting the property of the powerful 'upper' group from any form of attack or interference by members of the other groups. Where religion was concerned, the priests in the leading 'state' churches were generally from this 'European' upper group and the flock from the other. So the social reality was that the person at the lower end of the socio-economic continuum was black, had little formal education and was a peasant or unskilled labourer. He did not feel that social services (police and health for example) were his right and he generally belonged to a Revivalist (or Baptist) faith. On the other hand, the person at the upper end was white or mulatto, had secondary education, belonged to management, insisted on his rights – and sometimes on more than his rights – and worshipped at the Roman Catholic church or the Church of England.

Some writers seemed comfortable writing about the lives and

passions of those at the peasant end of the continuum, so we find their existence recorded in works like those of the playwrights Errol John (*Moon on a Rainbow Shawl*), Sam Hillary (*Chippy*), Douglas Archibald (*The Rose Slip*); novelists such as Roger Mais (*The Hills were Joyful Together*), George Lamming (*In the Castle of my Skin*), Andrew Salkey (*A Quality of Violence*), Samuel Selvon (*A Brighter Sun*) and Vidia Naipaul (*The Suffrage of Elvira*); and poets Louise Bennett and Barnabas Ramon-Fortuné. And not only were the literary artists telling the story. Their work was paralleled by the achievements of artists in other fields: the Trinidadian Beryl McBurnie in dance; Broodhagen of Barbados in sculpture; Baugh, the Jamaican, in pottery; and the calypsonians and early ska musicians. At the same time other writers spoke with passion of the life of those at the other end of the continuum. Geoffrey Drayton (*Christopher*) and Jean Rhys (*Wide Sargasso Sea*) exemplify this.

There were those whose work straddled the extremes, or who imaged the lives of those who lay between the extremes. There is also great variety in the work of these artists. The anguish of Derek Walcott (*Dream on Monkey Mountain*), the tentativeness of John Hearne (*The Autumn Equinox*) and the imaginative flight of Vic Reid (*The Leopard*) are all products of a kind of artistic mind that is purely Caribbean middle class.

Independence and now

Then came the era of Independence, beginning with Jamaica and Trinidad in August 1962. But the euphoria this phenomenon produced quickly faded in the glare of growing inflation, persistent poverty and a general feeling of frustration. People began to question the structure and goals of their society. A few took this to the logical extreme of total rejection of the society as a whole. Hippolyte's Jack in *The Drum-Maker* is the artistic archetype of the figure.

A number of factors had a profound effect on life in Caribbean society. The faith of Rastafari, with its rejection of the values of the western world and its suspicion of communism, spread through the region. Education became no longer a key to social mobility. Some societies began to experiment with new models of government and social organization. In the arts, people began to experiment with new forms: 'Dub' poets emerged, 'Sistren' the Jamaican women's theatre group, began to articulate the problems of working-class women, Rastafarian music began to affect the world with its sometimes violent, sometimes plaintive and, in people like Marley, always arresting protest at the condition of the poor in the Caribbean. Even religion was affected with a new 'Caribbean' theology being articulated by the new breed of churchmen.

So the artist in the Caribbean lives in a society full of conflict. It is also a society full of music, of rhythm, of the earthy warmth like that found in plays such as Bully's *Good Morning Miss Millie*. It is a society marked by linguistic variety as well. The artist has a wide range of sources from which to draw – hence the wide range of types of play in anthologies like this.

A brief history of Caribbean drama

Before 1930 we had no 'Caribbean' drama to speak of. The black population brought with them from Africa and India rituals and revelries which had by then evolved into something unique, but this could hardly be labelled as 'Caribbean drama'. The ruling classes, too, had their forms of theatrical entertainment, but this could not be labelled as truly Caribbean. The drama was to evolve together with the society.

The black peasants participated in many folk activities that were to have an influence on the development of a Caribbean theatrical style. Cannes Brulles had developed into carnival in Trinidad, while in Jamaica and the Bahamas John Canoe flourished. Tea meetings and 'pleasant-Sunday-afternoons' had grown into a strong cultural form in many of the islands, and dramatic religious rituals still held sway in the folk religion of the region. Indeed these are but a few examples. The islands were throbbing with a folk culture that was very often 'performance' oriented.

Of European theatre, on the other hand, there was also much evidence. Jamaica had a public theatre in 1682, Barbados had productions by 1729 and a theatre by 1812, Antigua had a theatre in 1788, St Lucia in 1832. Trinidad had three theatres by 1820. Most of the plays that were produced were European, although a few locally written plays were staged. But, even in the latter case, the writer, the cast and the audience were generally from the small upper class and the plays differed little in content and style from their European models.

In the first three decades of the twentieth century the growing middle class of educated blacks and mulattoes were inclined, as a result of their education, to gravitate towards the forms of theatrical entertainment of the ruling minority, although their natural inclinations often drew them to the revels of the majority. In the 1930s and 1940s this group began to produce the first plays that could truly be called Caribbean. The Jamaicans Una Marson (*Pocomania*), Tom Redcam (*San Gloria*), Frank Hill (*Upheaval*) and Roger Mais (*Hurricane*) had all written plays with this distinct flavour. Archie Lindo was the most successful playwright of the era, having written four well-received plays during this period. At the other end of the archipelago, in Trinidad, C. L. R. James, Arthur Roberts and Wilson Rogers were also working successfully in this new field.

The years between these early beginnings and the 1960s were marked by rapid development of this genre. The era saw the birth and growth of the Little Theatre Movement in Jamaica, the Whitehall Players in Trinidad, the St Lucia Arts Guild and other smaller groups throughout the region. In this era the Walcott brothers emerged and Douglas Archibald and his brothers flourished.

The tension that existed in the arts between the folk and European forms mirrored the tension that existed between the ways of life of the folk and those of the educated middle class. The works of Derek Walcott, who emerged in the 1960s, epitomize the result of this dual parentage of Caribbean drama – and the 'creative' conflicts that it often produced. His powerful *Dream on Monkey Mountain* probably explains more about some aspects of the tensions in society and the anguish of the middle class than all that the sociologists have written. His later play, *The Last Carnival*, gives a stark insight into the nature of the alienation of the French-creole elements in the upper class. It is interesting too that this play is a rewrite of the earlier *In a Fine Castle*, in which Walcott attempted to treat not only

French-creoles but also the young middle-class black revolutionaries of the late 1960s.

The decade of independence – the 1960s – saw a surge in creative activity. In these years Barry Reckord, Trevor Rhone, Dennis Scott, the Walcott brothers, Errol Hill and all of those more recognizably 'West Indian' writers developed their craft. Derek Walcott, the territory's leading playwright, teamed with an exciting and talented group of dramatists and formed the Trinidad Theatre Workshop. The Barn Theatre was established in Jamaica and premiered many of the works of the young Trevor Rhone. Guyana built its National Theatre at this time as well – signifying the general burgeoning of the art form there.

International recognition of the art form was also growing. Errol Hill's *Man Better Man* was performed at Yale while Errol John's *Moon on a Rainbow Shawl* was produced in New York, featuring some of America's finest young black actors – including James Earl Jones, Cicely Tyson, Kelly Berry and Ellen Holly.

By the 1980s this new generation of playwrights had honed their craft both into an incisive weapon against the foibles of our society and an instrument with which they could examine and explore the nature of our culture and our life-style. A number of other young artists had also begun to write, continually experimenting and testing the art form's ability to serve as this weapon and this instrument. A variety of drama styles became clear. These range from the burlesque folk comedies of Ed Bim Lewis (in Jamaica) and Freddie Kissoon (in Trinidad) to the experimental works of Dennis Scott, Rawle Gibbons and 'Sistren' (the all-female Jamaican group which does documentary theatre); the 'actors theatre' of Ken Corsbie and Mark Mathews in Guyana; the powerful commentaries of younger writers like St Lucia's Kendel Hippolyte; and the slick, crisp, commercially oriented works of Trevor Rhone.

In every territory one sees evidence of the movement of the art. In some, one man – like Bully in Dominica – seems to be the driving force, in others many persons work at it, in isolation or in collaboration with kindred spirits. The form is developing; this book indicates some of the ways in which this development is taking place.

2 Reading the plays

To the teacher

Plays as literature

Because of the constraints placed upon them by schedules and syllabuses, teachers are often tempted to approach any play that is set as a literature text in the same way as they would a novel or a short story.

But it is likely that a great deal may be lost through this approach, as it ignores those features of a play that make it a unique art form. In implementing it, we allow ourselves to ignore the fact that a playwright's art is quite different from that of the novelist; unlike a novel or short story a completed playscript is still 'unfinished'. There is another stage which the script needs to go through before it becomes, in the strictest sense of the word, a 'play'.

Even the playwright, in the throes of creation, is constantly aware that his playscript needs to pass through other artists before his intentions are truly achieved. (His intention, we would assume, is for the play to be produced on stage.) For this reason he often describes, in some detail, the set and stage properties that he thinks are most appropriate for conveying his message. He thinks of the use of space and the general impact of the colours, shapes and lines on the stage when it is set for the play.

The author also bears in mind movement and groupings — which often help to make statements about the characters in the play and their relationships with each other. We should, then, bear these in mind when treating the script as a class-room text; otherwise we would only be dealing with a part of what the writer has created.

There are other considerations that may affect our general approach to the teaching of plays. How do we deal, for example, with the tendency for there to be little direct authorial comment in the script? In a novel or short story, the writer, if he so wishes, can describe and comment at length on the changes or developments in the personality of each character. The playwright, however, must treat this largely through statements made by other characters in the play, by the speech and actions of the character and the actions of others towards him.

You may be able to call to mind occasions when you and your students tried to understand the elements of personality and character that a playwright revealed about a given individual in this way. This exercise is often followed by an attempt to draw conclusions about the fundamental characteristics of the protagonist and the way in which these changed during the course of the action of the play.

In this book, our suggestions and exercises carry this approach to the teaching of plays a little further. The teacher, we suggest, should assume the attitude of a part-time director. Like the director working with a cast, he works along with his class to attempt to discover the author's exact meaning and his intentions. He then considers, with his 'technical crew' (again the class), ways in which the set, stage properties and costumes would heighten a potential audience's understanding of, and response to, the play. Together they study the significance of the stage directions and the suggestions for lighting and sound effects.

The questions and suggestions that accompany each play in this book are structured so as to encourage teachers to dramatize as much of the play as possible. You may find that the discussions which surround an interpretation of a line, or the comments on the grouping of characters in the playing space available, may result in a deepening of your students' appreciation of the play.

A basic outline of the approach suggested is:

1. Everyone should get a broad overview of the play – its characters, its plot, its 'rhythms'. So start with a quick reading of the complete play. During this reading, there should be as few interruptions by the teacher (for comments and explanations) as possible.

2. In order to have students appreciate the approach – that is 'we are going to do this play' – work out a set design. Often this means adapting the design suggested by the author to the realities of the space available and devising ways of using desks

and chairs to represent other bits of furniture.

3. 'Block' each scene, using the actors you have assigned to the roles. Discuss, while doing so, the effect of the blocking so that everyone is sure of why the various moves have been made. (To 'block' is to work out the movement ana grouping of the actors on the stage.)

4. While working on each scene, discuss anything that is considered significant either by you or by any of the cast or crew. Even: 'But the costume we decided upon cannot work if she is to turn a cartwheel' is an important observation, since you may have decided on that particular costume because you felt that it said something important about the character.

5. Discuss the costuming. While doing this students can be encouraged to investigate the significance of the colour and style of each major character's costumes.

6. Concentrate on enjoyment. The creative and intellectual work that goes into this kind of endeavour can provide a lot of satisfaction – and fun. Actors (and students) work more creatively when they are enjoying themselves. We, as teachers, should ensure that we enjoy it as well.

If this programme sounds like the first two or three weeks of rehearsal for a production, this is deliberate. Treating it in this way gives the students the type of insight that performers and technical crew usually acquire while working on a play, and this should justify the approach. In encouraging this kind of insight, we also bring them closer to the playwright's original purpose.

Plays for playing

One of the main aims of this anthology is to make available some new Caribbean plays for performance by school groups and amateur theatre companies. We hope that these plays, though sometimes challenging, will help to remedy the situation which exists at the moment, where school and amateur festivals are affected by the fact that so few good Caribbean plays are available.

You will see that, accompanying each play, there are production notes in which suggestions are made to the director, in the hope that they will serve as a useful guide. Even if you are an inexperienced director, it is quite likely that you will still wish to attempt some things which are not suggested here. We urge anyone directing a play to be creative. In most cases there are many other ways to create the reality of the play apart from the ones we have suggested. If you have theatre experience, we hope that some of our suggestions will trigger some really excellent work on your part.

The anthology focuses on three aspects of play-directing. First, the idea that the director is a sort of acting coach is seriously pursued. Some of the questions that may be used to coax good performances out of young actors are given. Again, you may wish to add to, change or omit some of the questions, but we hope that they will serve as a guide.

Secondly, suggestions are made as to the staging of each play, and you may find the recommendations on groupings and movement useful. They are given because in all of the plays in this anthology one of the key elements to a successful production is 'rhythm'. *The Ritual* is a good example of a play that needs to be performed at the correct rhythm. The pacing of the scenes should be carefully worked out. Different scenes should be taken at different paces in order to give the play the needed variety as well as to capture the 'reality' in the scenes. Generally the movement in the play should be brisk and the actors should aim at that Trinidadian lilt in their speech but at a speed, a tempo, that never flags. If you aim at an energetic, brisk overall production and also for variation between the mini-scenes that run through the play, you should be able, using your judgement, to arrive at the correct balance.

Thirdly, set and costumes are considered. The plays were chosen with festival-type performances in mind. You may have noticed that apart from *Good Morning Miss Millie* the plays are all written for performance with the barest minimum of set and stage properties. At the same time, whatever is put on stage is either flexible or symbolic or both.

Costumes are seen as important as well. Often in these plays costume does not only say who the person is (as in Miss Millie) but it can say other things about the character. In *The Crime of Anabel Campbell*, for instance, you can hold a serious discussion on Dimity's and Ms Campbell's costumes – in terms of both colour and shape. While discussing this you will need to bear in mind how the colours you choose will show up against the red which dominates the set at the moment of the two characters' meeting. The idea that people's choice of clothing is a reflection of their personality can be used to help (a) costume the character and (b) discuss new facets of the character.

We hope that these considerations will help to improve the overall quality of your production.

Teaching plays as theatre-pieces

The 'practical' approach is encouraged throughout the anthology. In order to follow this you may need to leave the classroom to find a more suitable space. If the school hall is available at a convenient time, good use can be made of it. Here are some suggestions as to how to use this relatively large space for your class activity.

Before leaving the classroom, organize details of roles and responsibilities. When they arrive in the hall, the students should sit in the first few rows of the auditorium and together go over the plan of action for that day. If the activities are directed from the back of the class, you can avoid some of the problems that crop up when students are sent from their confined classroom into the openness of a school hall. You are also able to operate as a director often does: guiding, asking questions, making suggestions and observing the action while sitting in the audience. This can be very useful as it may help to focus the students' minds on the importance of the *performance* element of a play.

It is while you are in the hall, using a stage and treating the play text as a script being transformed into a play for performance before an audience, that you can focus on the details that a 'dramatic reading' in the classroom would miss. You may have the experience that play directors often have, of discovering many levels of meaning to the play which were hidden before they were treated in three dimensions on a rehearsal stage.

Another activity which students may enjoy, and which may be rewarding, is the making of cardboard models. In groups, students may be asked to make scale models of the stage of a nearby theatre. Many theatre managers would be quite willing to give the measurements (or a ground plan) of their stages. If none is available, you can invent the dimensions of an imaginary stage. When their models are made, they can then proceed to design the set for the play they are studying and finally to execute it, to scale, on their models.

Their attempts may not be professional, and their models may be rough. But the exercise also encourages them to consider the structural elements of the play – scene changes, the use of different areas of the stage for different scenes, and so on.

This practical approach need not take longer than the more sedentary analysis in the classroom. Every one of the students' decisions on apparently technical aspects of the play needs to be justified in terms of the playscript. As a result, the sessions spent sitting in class painstakingly perusing lines for hidden meaning may not be necessary. One can also use the practical activity as an incentive for the students to read the relevant sections of the play carefully in preparation for the class-time activities.

The choice of plays

These plays are all written by young Caribbean writers who are actively involved in the theatre scene of their various territories.

Dennis Scott has already established himself as one of our leading writers. He has produced two volumes of poetry and his work is widely anthologized. His plays are also well received. He was a teacher and then director of the Jamaica School of Drama. *The Crime of Anabel Campbell* is really the (classical) Clytemnestra story dressed in Caribbean garb. It calls for a small cast and only a minimal amount of stage setting. This melodrama is the kind that students can enjoy working on, as it is both mature in concept and technically challenging while not being out of their intellectual grasp.

Aldwyn Bully is Dominica's dominant figure in the area of drama. The early comedy *Good Morning Miss Millie* demonstrates two of Bully's strengths – his flair for vibrant dialogue and clear characterization. The play is the only rural piece in the anthology. It is also the only comedy. Unlike *The Crime of Anabel Campbell* it calls for a fairly large cast and, as such, is an ideal play for use by those schools and groups with a large number of students who want to go on stage.

The Drum-Maker, another play with a large (or medium if you wish) cast, is written by one of the Caribbean's best young playwright-poets, Kendel Hippolyte of St Lucia. The play was written in Jamaica where Mr Hippolyte worked as a teacher.

Zeno Obi Constance is another talented young playwright. He wrote *The Ritual* for the students of the school at which he taught in Trinidad. It was entered in the Schools' Drama Festival and caused quite a stir. It was clearly the play of the festival, but while TTT (Trinidad and Tobago Television) were in discussion with the school about having it presented on national television, protests came in from persons who felt that some of the themes with which it dealt were too sensitive for portrayal through this medium. As a result the project was abandoned. This caused some controversy as many felt that a play as fine as this and which treated such important themes should have been given the widest possible exposure.

The plays in this anthology have been chosen because they are suitable both for classroom study and for performance by schools and amateur groups. Most of all they were chosen because students should enjoy working on them. Have fun!

To the students: studying a play

There is a difference between a novel, short story or poem – all three of which are written to be enjoyed by the reader without the intervention of any other artists – and a play, which is intended for performance before an audience and so involves actors, a director, a designer and so on. You cannot approach a play in the same way as you would these other forms of literature.

The language of the play

Because a play is meant for performance, the language of the play is meant to operate effectively as 'heard language'. This means that the lines (the words spoken by the characters) of the play are not necessarily written in a style that leads us to sit back, reread and savour them. What is significant is that in a well-written play the lines that each character speaks may sound very much like the everyday speech of the type of person he represents.

This does not mean that the language is not carefully crafted, for if the play is to be a work of art, all aspects of the work should reflect this; and the language, especially, should be more poignant or powerful than that of everyday use. So the successful playwright is often one who has been able to strike the happy balance between these two extremes.

In this anthology, each play is set in a different territory. In the Caribbean, the language spoken by the common man differs from territory to territory and you may notice this difference in the three creole plays in the collection. An interesting feature though, is that *The Drum-Maker* was written by a St Lucian, while he was living in Jamaica, for performance by a Jamaican cast. Again, in some scenes in *The Ritual*, the Trinidadian characters are attempting Jamaican 'Rasta' talk.

Social class is another factor that is responsible for differences in the language we meet in the plays. The urban middle-class characters of *The Crime of Anabel Campbell* speak what can be called 'Standard English'. So do the girls in *The Ritual* when they 'become' middle-class characters. This standard English speech is quite different from the rural creole of the villagers in *Good Morning Miss Millie*.

When reading the plays aloud you should try to see if you can get the feel of the different speech rhythms. Try for the racy verve of the Dominican peasant in *Good Morning Miss Millie*, the Trinidadian lilt of *The Ritual*, the Jamaican flavour of *The Drum-Maker*, and the varieties of tone and cadence that Mr Scott puts in the mouths of his characters in *The Crime of Anabel Campbell*.

A final suggestion: if you are familiar with Jamaican speech rhythms, here is something you can experiment with. When reading *The Drum-Maker*, look for those moments when the written words are not exactly what you think they ought to be—

as Jamaican creole. (This happens from time to time because
Mr Hippolyte's own St Lucian speech patterns sometimes
creep into the dialogue.) Speak the lines aloud, in a Jamaican
accent, and see if they work. This suggestion is made because on
one occasion when the play was staged in Jamaica, the
Jamaican cast played the lines exactly as Mr Hippolyte wrote
them and the concensus among the cast was that this did not
affect the 'truth' of the production.

The final bit of advice in this section then must be: when
reading these plays, read 'with your ears open'.

Action in a play

Dialogue is only one element in a play – and it need not be the
most important element. Drama is, after all, *action*, and
language is only one of the ways in which action can be realized
and conveyed. Movement and gesture play a vital part in
creating the life of the drama. The good writer is aware of this
and often suggests, in his script, some of the action that would
help to further enhance the meaning of the play. There are, in
fact, different levels of meaning in a play and in your second and
third readings you may come across things that you missed at
first.

But meaning involves other things as well. For, although the
dialogue in a play is obviously fundamental at a number of
levels, different levels of meaning can be conveyed by movement, body position, gesture, relationships between bodies on
stage, etc. An excellent example of this is in the scene in Mr
Dennis Scott's play *DOG*, which was used as the 'unseen'
passage in the 1982 CXC English 'B' examination. The visuals
in this scene are more important to its success than the spoken
words. Body language, body positions and the movement of the
actors in relation to each other add important details to the
story. This is not to say that the language is unimportant, but
because of all the drama that is built up by the non-verbal
communication on the stage and the significance to the
audience of the body positions and gestures on the stage, the few
words that are spoken burn with a tremendous intensity. This is
an example of the kind of mixture of poetry of language and

poetry of action that can illuminate a scene and add to our understanding of life.

After each play, there are notes on the text. These include general suggestions for the movement of the actors on stage. If you consider them carefully and also try, when reading the plays, to visualize what is happening, your reading should be more rewarding.

When visualizing what is happening in a play you should remember that the author conceived of the action as happening *on stage*. The positions of the characters on stage in relation to each other are important for establishing the relationships between these characters as well as for making other 'statements'. For example, you may meet a scene in a play where two major characters are on stage with a crowd of persons surrounding one of them, while the other stands aside coughing loudly. From the stage directions and other clues in the text, you will have to decide on the answer to the question: why is he standing aside coughing? The answer may reveal relevant information about the characters. Is he trying to attract the others because he is jealous of the attention that the other man is getting? Is he doing this to warn the others that someone else is coming? Is he coughing continuously to ensure that they don't turn to him to ask him any questions? Is he simply suffering from a cold? On another level, the questions may lead you to investigate the significance of the stage picture – one man surrounded by a crowd, laughing, the other standing alone, coughing. (The man standing alone may be wealthy and handsome, the other may be poor and physically ugly; think of the statement being made here.)

Let us look at another kind of example, this time from one of the plays in this anthology: the moment in *The Crime of Anabel Campbell* when Dimity makes her first entrance. The body positions, the simultaneous utterance of the one word 'Johnny' by both Dimity and Anabel, the way the characters on stage look at each other, and the way they react physically to each other at that moment, all add up to a statement that a novel would probably need as much as a long paragraph to communicate. But the playwright is aware of the visual impact of the moment and trusts his co-workers in the art – the director and actors – to make it work and communicate all the levels of meaning that are contained in that moment.

The advice then is: when reading these plays, keep that 'inner eye' open.

Close study of a play: the characters

One of the best ways of trying to 'come to grips' with a character is to constantly ask four questions: What does he want now (at this moment)? Why does he want it? How is he trying to achieve this objective? Why does he choose this way to attempt to achieve it? A further question will place the character's actions into the context of the whole play. This is: How do the statements he makes and the actions he does in order to achieve what he wants, affect the others in the play and the action of the play in general? In answering these questions you should try to collect all the evidence that is to be found in the text.

There is another question that you can ask yourself. This one helps to make the connection between the play as literature and the play as a performance piece. The question is: What is the dramatic effect of this moment?

In looking at a character more closely you may discover aspects of his personality that you didn't notice on first reading. In order to allow this growth in your appreciation to happen you should be careful, when reading a play for the first time, not to be too firm in forming your opinions of a character. Remember, as well, that when people undergo serious strain, or have an encounter that is traumatic, it can have a lasting effect on them. Since plays are often about people under strain or people involved in traumatic experiences, we should expect that some of the characters may undergo radical change during the course of the play. Try to look for this and, in your analysis, to work out the lasting and more fundamental character traits in each individual as well as those ways in which he or she changes.

The audience

A playwright shares the creative act not only with the play's production team, but, like all artists, with his audience. Some literary critics feel that consideration of the audience for which an author is writing is unnecessary but it is useful for you to bear in mind the fact that, very often, there are things which the writer leaves to the imagination of his audience. Sometimes he makes references which he expects his readers or viewers to understand. These references may be topical or refer specifically to the society in which he lives. This is especially true in a work that is satirical and, as such, requires a certain amount of 'reading between the lines'. You should remember this when reading a play.

Audiences expect the local writer of plays to be aware of various aspects of their culture, of the pressures their society is undergoing and of their general concerns. The playwright often responds to this. This may be one of the reasons why Shakespeare's plays about Rome seem at times to speak more about the English society of his day than about Roman society. In general, if a writer wishes his play to be well received, he will try to make it relevant to the lives of those people for whom he is writing. Although the major concerns of the play may be universal in scope (as they are in Shakespeare's Roman plays), the action of the play very often involves the day-to-day concerns of the audience for which it is written.

The playwright is also aware of the effect that the immediate audience reaction has on the actual performance of the play. You may have been at performances of plays yourself and noticed that when an audience is thoroughly involved in the occurrences on stage this communicates itself to the actors and results in even more convincing performances. When next you attend a play, go backstage after the performance and ask a couple of the experienced actors about this.

If the cultural and sociological considerations that influence the playwright are borne in mind, they may shed a little light on some things that seem difficult to understand. Would this scene, this sequence, this exchange, have any special effect on the audience that the writer is addressing? This is one useful question that can be asked. Here are a few examples of questions of this sort that might reveal a different level of meaning:

How would the people in an Elizabethan audience (who believed in witches and the supernatural) react to the opening scene of *Macbeth*?

How would a Jamaican audience respond to the stage setting of *Schools Out*, with the large 'Out of Order' sign dominating the staff room and with the door that leads to the headmaster's office perpetually shut?

How would a young Trinidadian respond to the treatment of the girl in *The Ritual* who befriends the Rasta?

Why does the Trinidadian Rasta speak in a dialect that does not seem 'Trinidadian'?

Questions which relate to the general social background of the play can also be useful. Here are some examples of these:

How much is appreciation of Dennis Scott's *DOG* deepened by an awareness of the social developments in Jamaica during the 1970s?

What were the reasons for the civil strife in Ireland which caused so much anguish in the play *Juno and the Paycock*?

How much are the solutions offered in the penultimate scene of Zeno Constance's *The Ritual* influenced by the political and social movements in Trinidad in the 1970s?

How far should the concerns underlying the action of *The Drum-Maker* be seen in the light of certain social and economic problems in the Caribbean – the experiments with new political and economic systems in some of the territories, the relationship between the small Caribbean states and the IMF, for example? A little research of this type is always useful.

Background information

Although the sociological background of a play is important it can lead to one danger that you should try to avoid. Don't focus too much on background information and on considerations that are not always vital to the appreciation and enjoyment of the play. If you find yourself tracking down a bit of information, or contemplating an aspect of the background of the play that doesn't help to clear up a difficult area or to increase your appreciation and enjoyment of the play – forget it. A lot of time can be lost this way. It is often just as unrewarding to try to track down the source for the plot, or to make a psychological study of character-types. You should try to limit background research to what is directly useful. If time is short and a sacrifice has to be made, opt for enjoyment and not information. It would be a pity if you allowed a play that was meant to be fun, or to be fascinating, to turn into a drag.

A final word

The main point to remember is that these plays are here for your enjoyment. The suggestions on language, on action, on character study and on background reading are all meant to help you to a deeper and broader understanding of the plays, hence an ability to enjoy them more completely. Avoid battering away at anything you find unrewarding. Above all, have fun!

Keith Noel

Part II: The plays

1 The Crime of Anabel Campbell by Dennis Scott

This play is an ideal one for a young director. The basic plot is interesting but not complex, while the characterization gives scope for some good acting. At the same time, one of the most significant features of this play is that it encourages the director to consider some other aspects of drama to which amateur groups often give little attention.

Set design is an example of this. It is almost impossible to avoid serious consideration of set design as an integral part of the creation of this play. The script insists on a simple, but highly functional set, and for some imagination in its use. The director and his actors are also encouraged to think of movement and the position of actors on stage as a way to create mood and effect. There are also places in the script where you can think about the effective use of silence. If you choose, the use of lighting design as something that provides more than illumination can also be considered.

A melodrama, the play is set in Jamaica although there is nothing to tie it there. The language of most of the actors is Standard English and the characters, though clearly drawn, have no idiosyncrasies that would place them firmly in any specific Caribbean territory. The reason for this may lie in the fact that, basically, this is the Clytemnestra story. (Clytemnestra was a famous figure in Greek literature, about whom many plays and poems were written in ancient times.)

The play is suitable for a school or theatre group that wishes to have a small cast, a director and a designer explore the ways in which they could reveal the deeper reverberations of a script that at first reading appears to be very simple. This is an ideal situation for a young director who wishes to develop his craft as well as that of his actors.

The Crime of Anabel Campbell

A play in one act

People

ANABEL CAMPBELL
JOHN CAMPBELL, her husband
DIMITY HUNT, his mistress
BERNARD MOSES, Sergeant of Police
A CORPORAL
ANGELA MOSES, spinster

The scene

Alternates between gaol and Mrs Campbell's home.

It is 8 p.m. A spot warms slowly on ANABEL (BEL), *half seen behind the bars of her cell.*

BEL: Johnny! Johnny! Where's my son? Why don't you let him come home? I promise, I'll be good. Johnny? Johnny?

A second spot reveals, a little dimly, the desk and chairs down left. The SERGEANT *sits still, hands on desk, staring at a large grey file. The* CORPORAL *relaxes with a pack of cards.*

CORP: Mrs Campbell, you want something? Mrs Campbell?
BEL: Who's that, Johnny? Johnny Campbell, didn't you hear me calling you? All across the sea, I called till my tongue was thick, mile after mile! Come here now, Johnny. (*whispers*) Johnny? (*listens*)
CORP (*shuffling slowly*): I suppose you get used to it…

24

He lays out for Patience. BEL *begins to sing sadly, 'When Johnny comes marching home'.*

Ace out. Red three, black four. Don't make it get you down, Sarge.

BEL: Did you use to read her my letters, Johnny? On Sunday evenings across the bed when it was too hot to play, did you read her my letters, Johnny?

CORP: Can I ask you a question, Sarge?

BEL: No answer? Did you read them together, both of you, my son and my husband? Didn't you read them with her, didn't you?

CORP: Is the same file you have there, Sarge? You going to learn it by heart, man! Uh-huh! (*satisfaction – an ace out*) Jack on Queen…Queen on King…

BEL: Oh Johnny my son, my husband Johnny! How could you?

CORP: Shut up nuh, woman! Sorry, Sarge… The boys say you know she before, Sarge. Is true? Funny thing how you should make the arrest like that. Man, a real crazy woman that. That's why I not getting married, you know. You cyan trus' dem. Woman? Humph! …Man, Patience is the hardest thing to win! But I promise Janie I would stop playing domino. No more four D… Four dark on a red five… Ramnarace lose four shilling the other day jus' playing three cents a game.

BEL: I'm thirsty.

CORP: All the same, he don't do nothing else excep' play from the time he reach the station in the morning.

BEL: Can I have some water?

BERNIE *looks at the* CORPORAL.

CORP: Every night she want something! Las' night she wake me up – I wasn't sleeping, you know – jus' sort o' catching a snooze – an all of a sudden –

BEL: Sergeant!

CORP (*going*): Boy, this is a hard life!

BEL: Sergeant, please, I'm thirsty! Could I have a little water?

BERNIE *moves a little.*

CORP (*off*): I coming, Mrs Campbell!

BEL: Do you hear me begging, Johnny? And I was such a proud woman.

CORP (*reappearing up right by cell*): I have the water here.

BEL: Where's the Sergeant? Where's Sergeant Bernard Moses?

CORP: Inside, ma'am.

BEL (*turning away*): Oh. … Can he come here a little?

CORP: He have to stay at the desk, Mrs Campbell. You want me to tell him something for you?

BEL: I won't keep him long. The Sergeant knows me, you know. Couldn't he spare a minute?

CORP: You want the water, Mrs Campbell?

BEL: I expect it's the same as usual – warm tap water.

CORP: Yes ma'am.

BEL: Then I don't want it! When will they move me out of here and into a decent place?

CORP: They taking you out in the morning, Mrs Campbell. (*starts to go*)

BEL: No! Please, I want somebody to talk to! Call the Sergeant, Corp! No, stay! (*he goes*) Moses! Moses!

BERNIE *listens.*

BEL: Come back, please! It's the dark, I get to talking to myself. The water! I'm thirsty! You've got to give me water if I want it, isn't that so, Sergeant? Even when I went to kill her and she asked for water I gave it to her. It's in the confession, don't you remember? …I'm thirsty!

BERNIE *snaps file open.*

BEL: Do I look like a beast? Why is everybody afraid? Why do you shut me away and then forget me?

CORP (*at desk once more*): There she goes again. (*sits and resumes his game*)

BEL: When the Judge says I sentence you, Anabel Campbell to hang by the neck until you are dead, will you still be afraid,

all of you? I'm not afraid! From the beginning, when I knew
what would have to be done, I wasn't afraid. And I'm quiet,
now, you see. It happened, and I sat and waited for the
police to come, didn't I? Then why don't you keep me
company? How am I different from you, except that you are
afraid, and I was not?

BERNIE *pours water from thermos. He goes out.* CORP. *watches silently.*

BEL: Sergeant Bernard Moses, is that you? I knew you'd come!
That Corporal is afraid of me – afraid, can you imagine?

BERNIE *appears before cell.*

BEL: And water! – Cold water! Why, it's as cold as the day we
went swimming together, Angela and you and I. Do you
remember? Of course you do! You said, I love you Bel, and
I said, what a silly, sweet boy! I couldn't tell you then, you
see, what I had decided.

BERNIE *turns his back.*

BEL: Oh, I've hurt your feelings again! I mustn't keep you.
Thank you for the water, Sergeant Bernard Moses.

BERNIE *doesn't move.*

BEL: Am I so monstrous, my Sergeant? It was a terrible thing to
do. But they had done me such a thing, and Johnny. And I
was such a proud woman!

*She takes his hands through the bars, slides slowly down to rest against
them, speaking.* CORP. *tired of Patience, leafs dispiritedly through file.*

It was a terrible thing they had done, I was never good at
forgiving, Johnny always told me so. And if he knew that,
why then, it was stupid of him to come home, bringing her.
It was as if they dared me to say anything, do anything. Oh,
Sergeant Bernard Moses, I gave them every chance, and

they would not see. Dimity and Johnny, Johnny and
Dimity, my son and my husband and – Dimity is such a
pretty name – Johnny, you shouldn't have brought her
back with you! Though I had cleaned the house and made
everything ready for you to come home to, and die.

BERNIE: That was the first thing we saw, really. How clean the
house was. As though it had been made ready for a festival,
or a wedding. We had moved all the furniture out to the
front of the house, except the large red carpet and the neat
desk in the corner. All day the rooms had been shining with
sunlight, with her red slippers under the bed, and pale red
curtains over the windows. Only the blood on the sheets
that covered the girl in the room that night spoilt it. And the
look of patience on their faces, as though they were waiting
for visitors. Empty and patient, both of them. Her leg was
twisted under her so that she seemed a little clumsy, and
her thick red neck was broken by the knives. But he was
straight and peaceful. There were, of course, no witnesses;
just some spots of blood on the hair and thighs of – – the
accused. Later, they compared this blood with that of the
man and it proved to be of the same type. But that was
much later.

CORP (*reading*): On the day the crime was committed, Sergeant
Bernard Moses and his Aunt Miss Angela Moses were
present at the home of the accused. Their testimony seems
to confirm the statement made by the accused. (*phone rings*)
Hello, Hell – Oh, yes, sir! No, sir. He's just stepped outside
for a minute. (*covering mouthpiece*) Sergeant! – Sorry, sir? Oh
no, sir! She quite all right, sir. The van will be along in the
morning to pick her up. Right sir, I'll tell him…Jus' a
minute, Captain. (*takes message on pad*) 'Sarg. Moses is to
post a guard near the cell to ensure that the prisoner do no
harm to herself.' Very good sir. (*replaces receiver*) Sergeant!
Da mean I cyan sleep tonight! Sarge!

*Moves off. Phone begins to ring again, while lights fade quickly and he
calls. Ringing continues in the dark.*

Bright afternoon sunlight. Bare room, huge red carpet, desk, chairs by the walls, French windows to verandah. Phone rings. ANGELA MOSES darts in and answers it.

ANGELA: Mrs Campbell's house, yes. Hold on! It's long distance from the airfield, Bel!

BEL *enters from outside, followed more slowly by* BERNIE *in shirt-sleeves.*

　　Hold on, please, she's coming! Here, do you think it's him?
BEL: Anabel Campbell…A message? Yes, I see. (*pauses*) 'I'm on the way, Bel.' Thank you. No. Thank you for calling. (*begins to hang up, then –*) Miss! How long ago did the plane land? Fifteen minutes. I see. Goodbye.
ANGELA: Bel! I'm so glad for you! We'll just finish the polishing quickly and leave. You won't want us here when he comes.
BERNIE: No, of course. We're almost finished, aren't we, Aunt Angela?
ANGELA: Bernie, you'd better wax. I'll fix the beds meanwhile and polish afterwards. How's the time going? Oh Lord, what did I do with the pins?
BERNIE: They're on the couch outside.
ANGELA: Are they? I could have sworn I'd given them to you, Bel! Groceries…Did you remember the butter dear? Of course, it's come already, how silly of me to forget. And the cake, I'll have to send it over later. It was three eggs, wasn't it?
BEL: Angela!
ANGELA: Don't say a word, I know I'm driving everybody wild, Oh Lord, I'm getting too old for homecomings! Bernie! Don't *stand* there! (*she flutters out, vaguely. – Their smiles fade*)
BEL: I shall want you to stay a little while, when he comes.
BERNIE: If you want it, of course. I've got the whole day off.
BEL: Yes, it's – – very convenient.
ANGELA: (*crossing stage swiftly*) The pillows! I'd better sun them for a minute or two. …
BEL: Bernie.
BERNIE: Yes.
BEL: Nothing. …

ANGELA: The pins, I knew I hadn't left them outside. Bernie
  dear, see if you can find them.
BERNIE: Yes, Aunt.
ANGELA: There they are! All over your lovely new carpet.
BEL: He'll want something to eat when he comes. (*makes no move
  to go*) My husband John always had a fierce appetite. He
  and my son. Today, especially, I must feed him well.
BERNIE: Bel! If there's anything I can do, if there's anything you
  need help with –

ANGELA *exits.*

BEL: Why, my dear, you and Angela have been more than kind
  already! I don't know what I would have done without you
  both!
BERNIE: Kind!
BEL: I must take a moment to freshen up properly before he
  comes. Let me fix you some sandwiches, you must be
  starving!

ANGELA *enters.*

ANGELA: Bernie! Hurry! Bel, you lazy thing, you just sit right
  down and polish these knives! There! (*going out*) Oh, I shall
  die in this heat!
BERNIE: What's wrong? Are you happy, Bel? Really happy? I
  watch you and feel as though you're outside of all the
  preparations. As though you only wait for the moment
  when he actually comes before you come really alive.
BEL: Bernie, please!
BERNIE: No, let me say it now! The room is clean, and the house
  stands here a little way from the corner like a white painting
  with the three of us frozen here in the frame of three o'clock
  Monday. And I feel that we're waiting for the arrival of
  John Campbell and when he comes the picture will move
  and we'll wake up with a terrible sort of life. Why is this,
  Bel? Why do you make me feel afraid today?
BEL: You're being very silly, Bernie. Shouldn't I be happy? My
  husband's coming home today. I'm an empty woman

without him, Bernie.

BERNIE (*quietly*): You needn't have been, you know that, Bel.

BEL: We said that we wouldn't talk of that again, you remember.

BERNIE: We have to! His coming won't change anything for me, Bel, you know that! So where do I stand now?

BEL: There's been no change.

BERNIE: Except that I can't feel that anything's safe – I can't even
say what I mean! It's as though there's nothing in the house except an enormous red carpet, waiting for someone to walk on it and wake us up. And though I love you, I can't do anything to make you smile. I'm a full-grown man, but I'm afraid, though there's nothing to be afraid of! Bel, why is this?

BEL: Listen, Bernard Moses, listen to me! My son went away and I died a little. And my husband left me and I died a little It's three years now I've been walking empty, and today I came alive again. From the moment I got up this morning, I felt my bones growing and my breath drawing sweet and strong. And as every moment passes I see my way clearer. When he walks through that door, I'll be sure, and till then don't ask me to see you here, for there's nothing I can think of except my husband and my son Johnny that he brings home today with him dead and burnt to fine grey ash in a clean jar.

ANGELA *enters.*

ANGELA: Lord it's hot outside, Bel! You haven't even touched them! Here, let me do it. I must look a mess, Bernie. The clock, set it to the right time, boy! Don't stand there! Oh, I'm dying of thirst! I'm getting old and lazy, I know that, there was a time I'd blow through a house and leave it clean as a whistle – lemonade, lemonade! That's what we need! Bel darling, if you're determined to stand there dreaming of your Johnny, why don't you make us something cool to drink? Oh my Lord, how the day has flown! I can scarce believe it's almost four already! Here, hurry on, you're only getting in the way, and there's a million and one things to do.

BEL *leaves*. BERNIE *turns to go*.

Bernie! Bernie! (*polishing vigorously*) I'm an interfering old woman. Everybody knows that. But Anabel is my friend. Whatever she decides to do, it's none of your business, you'll remember that, won't you?

BERNIE: I don't know what you're talking about, Aunt Angela.

ANGELA: I see. I don't know what's between you and I don't want to know but when Johnny Campbell comes home today, I don't want to hear of you hanging around this house like you've been doing for the last year.

BERNIE: Don't you think I've got my pride?

ANGELA: Anabel, she's got her pride too, you know. Don't make it any more difficult for her, boy. She has a lot of forgetting to do, and it won't be easy for a woman like her. ... If she says come and see us, come, but stay away from this house as much as you can, Bernard, once you deliver my cake this evening. I want no hate on your conscience.

BEL (*entering*): You both look very serious. What has happened?

ANGELA: My dear, the worm is turning. He's refusing to do any more work!

BERNIE: Aunt Angela!

ANGELA: Now, no more arguing, my dear, we'll just have to sharpen these knives. Bernie, take them all into the back and do something about those edges. Bring them back; I'll have to clean them again when you're finished. Come my dear, those table tops are breaking every bone in my back. How much time have we got left? I'm afraid we'll have to leave most of the furniture in the front gallery for the time being, we'll never get it all inside in time.

ANGELA *leaves. Lights fade. Spot warms on* BERNIE.

BERNIE: The knives were identified as belonging to the defendant, and the officer who discovered the body admitted that he himself had that day sharpened and cleaned them. The fingerprints on the blade and hilts were identified as those of the accused. At a quarter past

four on Monday the 14th a taxi deposited at the home of
Mrs Campbell two persons and their baggage. They were
John Campbell and Miss Dimity Hunt, a – friend. …So far
that day there had been nothing obviously wrong. …

Spot fades slowly on BERNIE *polishing knives. Warm general lighting.*
BEL *enters quickly with* ANGELA.

BEL: Bernie! There's a taxi coming up the road.

ANGELA: Do you think it's him, Bel?

BEL: Yes.

BERNIE (*from the door*): It's passed. False alarm.

BEL: No, it's him.

ANGELA: Let me look. It's turning! Come see, Bel!

BEL: I don't have to, Angela. I'd know him coming anywhere.

ANGELA: It's stopping here. … You're right! … He's greyer than
I remember him! Oh Bel, my dear! (*hugging her*) Quickly, fix
your hair, let him see you looking your best!

BEL: That's all right, Angela. Go, open the gate for him. (*she goes*)

BERNIE: There's someone with him! (*pause*)

BEL (*slowly*): Yes?

BERNIE: Bel, are you sure you want us to stay?

BEL: Yes!

BERNIE: We can come back in a little while, if you like. Wouldn't
it be better to meet him alone?

BEL: Is it a woman?

BERNIE: Yes.

BEL: Is she young? Beautiful? (*no answer*) …Yes.

ANGELA (*off*): Anabel! Are these all your bags? Oh John, you
look so distinguished now! (*laughter*) She's inside, come in,
come in!

BEL: Do they walk close together, Bernie? Do they? What are
they doing now?

BERNIE (*as in a dream*): He's paying the taxi – no! She's giving
him the money and smiling.

BEL: Oh yes, that's my Johnny, that's my Johnny. …

ANGELA (*off*): Come along – you too Dimity! – May I call you
Dimity? She's inside fixing her face, you know women! –
My dear, she'll have to feed you, you're nothing but skin

and bone! Bel! Bel! (*sings*) 'When Johnny comes marching home –'.

BEL *lays down the mirror and stands down left facing the door.*

BERNIE: Bel. ...

As the others enter their animation dies down, ceases.

JOHN (*off, laughing*): Angela! You haven't changed a bit, as flighty and gay as I recall. (*enters*)
ANGELA (*off*): Do let me take this, my dear, and your coat, Johnny. (*comes in*)
DIMITY (*off*): Thank you. That's very kind of you. (*comes in*)

For a moment nobody moves.

BEL: Johnny.

He starts forward into the room. DIMITY *holds him back.*

DIMITY: Johnny.
BEL: Welcome home, Johnny. Even with her, welcome, Johnny.
JOHN: Is this the way you greet me, Anabel – in black, as for a funeral?
BEL: Do you forget, Johnny? My son is dead. Welcome home.
JOHN (*to* DIMITY): Why are you shivering? This is my wife Anabel. ... This is Dimity.
BEL: I know.
ANGELA: Come .. Child. ...
BEL: Come. I have cleaned my house for you... .

He comes down to her slowly across the red carpet. Suddenly, there is movement everywhere in the room.

ANGELA: Lord, you must be tired. Bernie, draw up a couple of chairs – just draw them in from the wall. That's right. Sit down, my dear.
DIMITY: The carpet! It's so red!

ANGELA: I can't think why people travel by plane. In the days when I could still move from country to country it tired me so!

BEL: You haven't met. Johnny, this is Bernie, Sergeant Moses of the police force. My husband.

BERNIE: How do you do.

ANGELA: Remember, I used to speak about him, my nephew in Jamaica.

JOHN: This is Dimity Hunt. She was a friend of Johnny's.

BEL: How do you do, Miss Hunt. Any friend of my son's is welcome here.

DIMITY: Thank you, Mrs Campbell.

ANGELA: How formal we all are! (*nervously*) What can I do to break the ice? Let's see —

BERNIE: I really must be going.

ANGELA: Of course! A little something to eat and drink — what will you have?

JOHN: Dimity?

BEL: You must forgive me; perhaps you'd like to wash …?

ANGELA: Oh dear, this is terrible! Here am I behaving as if this was my house! Come along dear, I'll show you the way.

BERNIE: Aunt Angela! (*she stops*) Glad to have met you, Miss —

BEL: Hunt. She was a friend of Johnny's.

BERNIE: Bel, I'll be off now. If there's anything I can do —

BEL: How strange of you to say that!

JOHN: What's that, did I miss something?

ANGELA: This nephew of mine seems to think we're in the way. He's right of course. You just go straight along to the end of the passageway —

BEL: No, it's just that Bernie said I should call him if anything went wrong. …

DIMITY: I'll be all right, thank you. I've just got a slight headache.

JOHN: Is there anything she could take, Bel?

BERNIE: Did I say that?

BEL: In a moment. …

BERNIE: Bel?

BEL: I'm sorry, Bernie, what did you say?

ANGELA: Never mind; come, Bernie. Take care, darling. I'll call

later. I'm sure to have forgotten something! Goodbye
everyone, goodbye!

She leaves brightly, with BERNIE *following slowly.*

BEL: There's a bottle of aspirins in the cabinet over the basin.
Take a couple. Perhaps I'd better come with you—
DIMITY: No, don't, don't tou—Oh…I'll be well, thank you, I'll
soon be all right. …

DIMITY *exits, trembling. There is a pause.*

JOHN: Come, sit beside me, Bel. (*she does, watching him*)
BEL: How are you, John?

JOHN *looks at her, then past her to the passageway. Silence.*

JOHN: I haven't changed much, Bel. Maybe not at all.
BEL: Why did you bring her back, John? (*no answer*) I think I
could have forgiven you if you had not brought her back.
(*pause*) John. Will you send her away? Now. She will find a
place to stay. Will you, John? We will forget you ever
brought her here, into my house. John! I have my pride! Let
me forget her, and send her away!

DIMITY *enters unsteadily.*

DIMITY: Johnny? Where are you?
JOHN (*goes to her*): Here I am. Sit down, rest here.
DIMITY: Why is the room all red?
BEL: What's wrong with her?
JOHN: She gets these attacks sometimes. It's nothing. She only
needs to lie still for a few hours and the fever sweats itself off
her.
DIMITY: Let me go! Let me Go! The room smells of blood, I tell
you!
JOHN: Hush, Dimity! This is home!
BEL: Let her go, John. I'll call a taxi right now.
JOHN: Go? She can't go out like this!

BEL: You say it's not serious, why can't she wash her face and
    go? Angela would be glad to keep her. There are hotels!
JOHN: How can I? She's my responsibility, Bel!
BEL: Is she, John?
DIMITY: The whole house is like death. Shadows in every
    corner. .... John, John, where are you?
JOHN: Here, beside you, child. See, I won't leave you.
DIMITY: Johnny, has she gone?
JOHN: It's her house, dear. She's here with us.
DIMITY: Oh, send her away, please Johnny!
BEL: Send me away!
JOHN: Shhh! Come and lie down, Dimity.

BERNIE *enters, and stands apart.*

DIMITY: No. I must go! We've got to leave, John, the house
    smells of blood, don't you sense it?
JOHN: You're not well, that's all. It will pass. You'll sleep quiet
    when the fever breaks.
BEL: How dare you bring her here?
DIMITY: You'll lie beside me, John? You know I can't sleep
    without your hand by my neck.
JOHN: Dimity! You mustn't talk like that!
DIMITY: When he died I couldn't sleep for nights, you
    remember. I had grown so used to his coughing and his thin
    body beside me.
JOHN: Dimity, you must rest. She talks like that sometimes,
    wild, but she doesn't mean half of what she says. Dimity? – Sh
    burning with the fever!
BEL: Let her speak. Let my shame be complete.

Lights fade to dim. Spot full on BERNIE.

BERNIE: So she told them. About Johnny Campbell and his
    father, John, the two men she loved. And the woman whose
    son she had taken away, whose husband she had kept for
    herself when the young man had been drained dry, stood
    quiet and grew strong as the evening darkened. Later,
    when the Judge at the inquest tried to stop her from

repeating the tale, she could not stop. It was as if every
word Dimity Hunt had spoken were burned into her spirit
and could not be driven out. The man, John Campbell,
rocked the girl to sleep, and the carpet grew redder and
redder in the evening sunlight, until the girl slept cool and
quiet in his arms.

DIMITY: John? Are you here?

JOHN: Sleep, my love. Go to sleep. Is the room empty, the boy's
room?

BEL: Yes. Take her there. I shall soon come.

JOHN *leaves, carrying the girl.*

BERNIE: She followed him in her mind's eye down the corridor
and past her room, to the door beside it. Could she have
heard the door close behind them? Listening in the
courtroom we held close to reality with the sound of the
clerk's typewriter tapping gently the testimony of Mrs
Anabel Campbell. ... The key. It was there in his pocket.
Secretly, she opened the larger trunk, and took out her son.

BEL (*with urn*): John Campbell, my son. Can you hear me?
Welcome home, my son. You left me and I could do
nothing, for they say it is right that a man should leave his
mother and find other flesh. What did she do to chain you
so to her? Johnny? This woman with fine hands and the
sleek head? I know she gave you her body, Johnny, and that
I could not do. But what did she promise you, that could
make you go so quickly, one night off to her island? You,
sick already with a cold that would never heal? If you had
brought her home, I would have tried to understand, and
you need never have gone. ...

BERNIE: What was he doing, John Campbell, in the room with
the sleeping girl? Had he loosened her clothes, had he
covered her over in the dark house? What was he thinking
of, watching the girl with a hunger great enough to eat up a
man and his son?

BEL: Did you think of it first, Johnny? Or did she? Why didn't
you write to *me*? Do you think I would have turned you
away, knowing you were sick? All the time I wrote you,

telling you, come back, come back, Johnny, and she knowing you needed help, and sending nothing. Did you think I was mocking you, Johnny? Could you think I knew your desperate need and mocked you, Johnny? (*she listens, motionless*) And then I found the letters and faced him, and sent him off to find you. Before he went, you know what he said, Johnny? He said he had done it because he was jealous of you. Of you! Johnny, you were my *son*! (*long pause*) How long did it take you to die, Johnny? Two, three, four months? He never wrote to say. Did she leave your bed before you gave up the fight? Did she wait, Johnny? Johnny, I could have forgiven her that she brought you grief, even that she brought you death, Johnny! But to take my husband, your father, to her bed as though there should be no difference! As though whichever pleasured her it was all one. That both should share her womb! Oh, the shame, the shame! (*silence*) Surely, it must bring death. ...

Enter JOHN.

JOHN: What are you thinking of, Anabel, sitting with your son's ashes?
BEL: I am thinking, John Campbell, that my heart has dried and gone brown as old tamarind shells.
JOHN: She has gone to sleep. ... Will you talk with me, Anabel Campbell?
BEL: Let me set my house in order.

Pause. She takes up tray with cutlery, and leaves.

BERNIE: It is growing late in the courtroom. But even the Judge no longer fans the flies away, and the spectators are still, hearing to the dark, bitter end the testimony of the defendant. If there was a cry from the house, if there was time for the girl just to call out, recognizing at last the smell of her own blood on the clean sheets, we shall never know. Did he hear anything? It seems not. When she came back, Anabel Campbell, John Campbell had not moved from the red carpet that had that day welcomed death.

BEL *enters carrying her shoes. She comes to him. After a while, she smiles.*

BEL: Oh John.

JOHN: There is blood on your hand.

BEL: Didn't you hear me cry out? I cut myself on a knife. They were too sharp.

JOHN: Let me see it.

BEL: No! It is nothing! (*He takes her arm, nevertheless*) Oh John, it has been so long since you touched me. (*He lets her arm fall; she smiles*)

JOHN: How have you been, Anabel?

BEL: Lonely, John.

JOHN: What's his name, – Bernie?

BEL: You'd believe that? Of me? You think I wouldn't wait for you?

JOHN: Sometimes the flesh knows nothing of the heart's patience.

They are silent for a moment.

BEL: And you, John? Was she clever in the ways of your bed?

JOHN: Anabel! Don't talk like that!

BEL: Did she treat you well, John? … Oh, the nights I lay awake for you in my widow's bed.

JOHN: If I dared, I would say I was sorry. But it is not a thing to be lightly said to a woman who has been wronged as I have wronged you.

BEL: Say it nevertheless, John, say it.

JOHN: Bel, you know how hot I always was. I never learnt the control you had. Any temptation was a hunger for me, you know that, Anabel!

BEL: My poor John! (*tenderly*) I know. And now I have so much love stored up for you, my dearest.

JOHN: Can you feel that way about me still? I didn't want to hurt you, Bel.

BEL: Don't talk, Johnny. … My poor Johnny, soon all our debts will be paid.

She has drawn him down to the carpet.

JOHN: Oh, Bel, Bel.
BEL: Don't torture me, Johnny! It's been so long…

He turns her and begins to unfasten the buttons of her dress at the back.

JOHN: Let's go in.
BEL: I can't wait, Johnny, oh my son, my son.

The lights begin to fade.

JOHN: I should have come back sooner.
BEL: Yes.

Blackout, then tight spot bright on BERNIE.

BERNIE: On the bright red carpet in the hot dark, John
      Campbell loved his wife Anabel for the last time. What strange
      sickness possessed her we cannot say. …. When they had
      finished and his body lay hot and sated beside her, Anabel
      Campbell, with the knife she had used for Dimity, killed
      him.

As lights warm slowly, BEL *turns to us, and we see the red knife. The phone
rings. Eventually she moves to it, answers it.*

BEL: Yes, Angela. No, just a little tired, my dear. No,
      everything's quiet. … Cake? Oh, yes. …. Yes, it was three
      eggs. Yes, I'm sure it will be very good. You're sending
      Bernie round with it? Thank you. I see. Yes, I think I hear a
      car outside. It's probably Bernie. Thank you, my dear.
      Goodbye, goodbye. …

*She replaces the receiver gently, and begins to hum 'When Johnny Comes
Marching'. Walks slowly towards door.* BERNIE *enters slowly. She leans on
him, beating time to the tune with her fists. She slides down to the floor,
holding his arm. He steps forward into the room, she holding him. The
bars lower slowly between them. General lights fade, except for spot which*

lingers on them while another spot warms on desk. Phone rings, and continues ringing till answered.

BEL: Johnny? Johnny? 'When Johnny comes marching home…'
CORP (*off*): Sergeant? Sergeant! Captain just called, sir. Guard on the cell all night, sir!
BERNIE: Thanks. I'll answer it.
CORP (*appearing up by cell*): Stay here, Sarge?
BERNIE: No, she'll be all right for a while. (*answers phone*) Sar'nt Moses speaking. Yes, sir. I'll call if she seems to need a sedative. Very well, sir. Goodnight! (*sits at desk looking at folder*)
CORP (*shuffling*): Play gin rummy, Sarge? (*no answer*) Sarge?

BERNIE *gives a slight shake of his head.*

CORP (*lays out for Patience*): Any time you ready I going fix a chair by the cell, Sarge.

Pause. BEL *starts singing again. He listens for a moment, shrugs, continues playing.*

CORP: Two on three, three on four on red five… turn over, Jack on red Queen on black King…

He's stuck. Sighs. Begins to deal himself threes. He continues playing quietly until the lights are down and out.

CURTAIN

Questions for the Class or Cast

1. (page 25) Why was the Corporal playing solitaire/patience? What effect/impression should this have on the audience? How would his body language, and so on, help to create this effect?
2. (page 25) Why does the Sergeant ignore Bel's cries?

3. (pages 24–5 The Corporal, noticing how Sergeant Moses seems to be ignoring Bel's cries, says 'I suppose you get used to it', yet a little later on he says 'don't make it get you down Sarge'. What has the corporal realized (or understood) about the Sergeant, here?

     What could an actor, playing the Sergeant, do to make it clear to the audience that he is not actually 'used to it' and that it finally starts to get him down – without committing an 'acting cliché'?

4. (page 25) When the Corporal first talks about himself he says 'I not getting married, you know', and then shortly afterwards says 'I promise Janie I would stop playing domino'. What is the irony here? What do we learn of the Corporal in these statements that could be of help to an actor playing this role? On pages 25 and 28, the Corporal again has what seems to be 'lighter' lines, for example: 'last night she wake me up…I wasn't sleeping you know' and 'Da mean I cyan sleep tonight'. What do we learn here about the Corporal's function in the play that can help an actor in playing the role?

5. (page 28) Why does the playwright refer to the Sergeant as 'Bernie' (when indicating that he is the speaker) and not by his rank as he does in the case of the Corporal?

6. (page 26) 'When will they move me out of here and into a decent place?' What does this say about Mrs Campbell's mental state?

7. (page 26) Bernie 'snaps file open' – why does he keep reading the file? Think first in terms of characterization and then in terms of the practical staging of the play.

8. (pages 25–6) Why does the Sergeant not go to Bel as soon as she calls him?

9. (page 27) Is the Corporal afraid of her? Support your answer.

10. (pages 26–7) Why does Bel keep repeating: 'I was a proud woman'? Was it hurt pride that drove her to her extreme action?

11. (page 28) Why does Bernie say that the bodies had a 'look of *patience* on their faces'? What reverberations does this word have?

12. (page 28) Why did the playwright choose to have the carpet and curtains red (and to stress it)?

13. (page 29) Why is Angela so anxious/jittery when we first meet her?

14. (page 30) Angela says, 'Oh I shall die in this heat!' (a) what is the irony here? (b) What is the significance of 'heat'? (c) How can the physical surroundings be made to seem hot?

15. (page 30) Bernie says to Bel: 'As though you only wait for the moment when he actually comes before you come really alive.' Discuss the dramatic significance of this line.

16. (page 30) Bernie says 'Why…Bel? Why do you make me feel afraid today?' How much can this be an actor's cue – informing the actress playing Bel about what her action should reveal/conceal? Is the audience to feel, then, that she had planned it all? (In considering this the actors/class should bear in mind her statement on page 28 which ends: '…though I had cleaned the house and made everything ready for you to come home to, and die'.) Did she then have an 'If he…I will' plan?

17. (pages 34–5) When it is clear that Dimity has come with John, Angela says and does quite a few 'surface' actions. Try to identify all of the things she does. What is she really trying to do at each point? What does the reader/actress learn about Angela from her actions during this moment in the play?

18. (page 35) What is the effect of John's line: 'she was a friend of Johnny's' on everyone else?

19. (page 35) The through line of the conversation between Bel and Bernie evolves around Bel's interpretation of Bernie's line. 'If there's anything I can do…' She says that he had suggested she call him if anything went wrong. Why is this? Did she really mishear? What is happening to Bel?

20. (page 36) Why does Dimity say 'No, don't, don't tou…'? What is the effect of this? Why is her behaviour to Bel so strange at this point? Or is it? (Bearing in mind how Bel may be acting at this point?)

21. (page 39) Why would John be jealous of his son? What does this tell us about him and/or about Bel? Does it help to explain why he had an affair with Dimity? Was it because of

Johnny? Because of her frailty? Or because something else in his personality?

22. (page 42) As an actress would you sing the final 'When Johnny comes marching home' or speak it? (Consider the effect of each.) If you chose to sing, what rhythm would you choose for the song?

Production notes

This play is suitable for those who prefer to work with a small cast on a tight, intense drama. It gives the opportunity for a small group of actors to explore in great detail the social, psychological and physical factors that make a character 'tick'.

Each of the characters is an enigma and a young actor should find it fascinating digging below the surface of the script to find all of the things she/he would need to make the scripted character into a living person.

The teacher/director can help by asking questions that would lead the young actors into a deeper insight into the personalities that they are bringing to life: always 'why does he/she say that?' 'What does he want here?' 'In the light of …(x) … why does she say/do …(y)…?

Set design

The playwright has created a work which eliminates one of the main problems that often face a low-budget production – the vexing question: where does one get an appropriate set?

Although the action moves between a gaol cell, a police station front office, and a middle-class living room, the play is written in such a way that the action flows from one set to another with minimum problems of set-changes.

The structure of the play also calls for the living room to be cleared of all furniture except for a few chairs and a desk, which can (should) be the same desk used in the police station set.

Although the script (page 41) calls for the cell-bars to be lowered between Bel and Bernie this can be altered if the performing space does not allow for it. There are at least three possible alternatives: (a) a short blackout during which a frame with upright bars can be brought on; (b) in a production that uses some stylization the bars can be brought on by the crew (or cast), moving in a stylized manner; (c) the director may opt for no bars at all. A mark on the floor, a pool of light, or something of that sort may designate the cell area. The onus then is on the actor to create the feel of the cell using his body. This type of production, when it works, tends to be the most satisfying to director, cast and, most importantly, audience.

As is mentioned above, the writer has gone two-thirds of the way as far as design for this work is concerned. The design is intrinsic to the play's mood and, for this reason, Mr Scott has made it clear that he would like a sparse, almost bare stage setting. It may be interesting to contemplate the effect of this on an audience. For example, one may ask: 'Does the emptiness of the living room tell us anything about the inhabitant of the house now that she has been living alone? This may lead us to consider the writer's stage setting and stage directions again. Are they put in solely to make it convenient to move from one playing area to another, or is there more to it than this? Even if a director decides to see them as being put in simply to facilitate the shifts of locale, the challenge here could still be to use this set in such a way as to suggest to the audience something about the lives of the inhabitants of the house. The use of as few pieces of furniture as possible, carefully blocked scenes and clever lighting can add a dimension to this play that may be very interesting. Emptiness; a void; human beings' inability to fill 'space' between each other; a 'cold' empty house/home (especially one that glows with a hot red colour); empty sterility – these are a few of the ideas and images which can be discussed with the cast/class and even experimented with during rehearsals.

The playwright also suggests a dominant colour – red. But when one considers that a lot of the play is enacted in a police station and gaol cell, one realizes that one has to play other colour/moods against it. The director (or the class) can discuss the use of these colours and moods and the effect they will have.

Lighting

Lighting (where available) helps tremendously. If one wishes to experiment with lighting to establish scenes and moods, there are a number of possibilities. One may, for example, move from a dimly lit stage at the start, with spotlights picking up the main playing areas, to full floodlights on the transition to the house (especially with some orange and a little red gel added). This is but one of many possibilities – the director will find the ideas flowing when he or she decides what images to present, what moods to create, what subtle messages to transmit.

Costumes

Deciding on costumes for a play like this seems easy, but careful choice can help to create 'reality' more convincingly. In the first instance one must create reality on the level of 'What would Bel wear on this occasion?' What colour? Cut? Design? 'How would Bernie dress?' In uniform? If so, would he visit Bel wearing his uniform? If not, in what? How sober, sombre (or flashy), a person is he? What about the others? Is John a bit of a dandy or is he a simple dresser? How would Dimity dress to travel? These and other questions have to be asked and answers can only be found after a great deal of thought has gone into creating the characters. The director/actors should bear in mind, though, that the clothes a person wears help to create that person. (It indicates the picture he would like the world to have of him and this tells us something about his personality.) It follows then that a character's clothes should be decided upon during the course of the rehearsals – not at the beginning or thrust upon the actor on dress-rehearsal night. Teachers who are studying a play as a literary text with a class can also usefully undertake the type of character-analysis that costuming a play requiries.

The other level of reality that needs to be considered is one which is more subtle. The question to be asked is often a vague 'does it feel right?' Do the cut, colour and design of the costumes help to create that mood/feel/atmosphere which makes the play come alive? Another consideration is that costuming a person in a way which clashes strongly with the ambience of the set may make a statement about the relationship between the character and the rest of the persons in the play – who may blend perfectly into the setting – or between the character and the setting itself. The converse is also true.

Another point is worth mentioning here. Set, costume and lighting design should be worked on together – or at least when each of these is being discussed the others should be borne in mind. Here is an example of the kind of problem that can ensue if one does not.

A director may decide, for some good reason, to clothe a character like Dimity in a colour which is soft (say, to avoid giving the impression that she is in any way a 'scarlet woman'). So the director and the person in charge of costumes choose a cool pastel shade – a beige or cream for instance. But at another time the director and the set designer had carefully chosen the right colour of the room to set off the red carpet – a cream or cleverly mixed shade of beige. On dress-rehearsal night, when the set has been painted and the costumes are fitted – all is set – Dimity enters, and fades into the woodwork! Her costume and the walls are exactly the same colour (and Dimity may even be a pale brown girl). In the bright stage light everything upstages her! This underscores the need for a stage production to be the result of close teamwork.

Some Points to Consider

The characters: the underlying implications

There are a number of interesting twists which have been cleverly crafted into the plot. They bear close observation. An example of this is the fact that it is Angela (pages 30 and 32) who gives Bel the knives, then takes them from her and gives them to Bernie for him to sharpen. (It is almost as if she places the idea in Bel's mind and then incriminates Bernie.)

The dramatic moments

There are a few moments in the play that must be carefully considered. If played well, they can help to add the extra magic that contributes to any play's success.

One such moment occurs on page 34 when John Campbell has just entered the house. Both Bel (who is in front of him) and Dimity (who is close behind him) call to him by name, 'Johnny'. Players and director (or teacher and class) would do well to consider the general effect of this moment.

Another of these moments is that created by the verbal response of the persons on stage to the news that Dimity 'was a friend of Johnny's' (page 35). Persons working on the play should consider what the non-verbal response/reaction to this would be.

Clues of characterization

There are clues as to the details of character, motives and motivation scattered all over the pages of most playscripts – and this one is no exception. Consider for example: Johnny suspects Bel of having an affair with Bernie (page 40).

JOHN: How have you been, Anabel?
BEL: Lonely, John.
JOHN: What's his name, – Bernie?
BEL: You'd believe that? Of me? You think I wouldn't wait for you?

What does this suggest to us about: (a) John's personality; (b) the relationship between the two; (c) John's feelings about his affair with Dimity; (d) Bernie's actions/reactions to Bel when John was present; (e) Bernie's response to John; (f) Bel's attitude to John, to Bernie and to her marriage?

Other examples of these 'clues' are suggested elsewhere in these notes.

2 *The Ritual* by Zeno Obi Constance

The Ritual, although basically symbolic, has a storyline which is easy to follow and which ties together the various elements of style and plot.

Five schoolgirls are waiting in a classroom for their teacher, who is attending a staff meeting. After a brief introduction to the situation in which we learn that Omega is pregnant, the play traces the events which led up to the pregnancy and to Omega's arrest for prostitution.

The five girls alternate as the various characters who are involved in Omega's story. As Mr Constance says, 'they also take turns in becoming Omega, whose guilt they carry, in an effort to cleanse themselves of Omega's burden – which they bear – and to better understand and appreciate the problems and feelings of the Caribbean woman whom Omega symbolizes. As a result they have no names, only numbers, until the very end'.

Issues that are important to Caribbean youth come into focus. Among them are: Rastafarianism (the baby's father is a Rastaman); the generation-gap, which exists between Omega and her parents; parenting, as witnessed in the confused, clumsy attempts at bringing up a family that the parents display; the police and their attitude to youth (on slim evidence they arrest Omega for prostitution); and the inadequacies of the legal system. All this results in a kind of documentary theatre, the elements of which are tightly interwoven in the well-knit storyline.

The play is sub-titled *Friday Morning – First Period* since at one level the action takes place on any Friday morning during the first period. This is the base to which the performers return after each episode or ritual. This is the symbolic level to the documentary. The writer makes statements about the Caribbean woman, the burden she bears and the hopes she carries

51

forward. He also suggests directions in which the society may look for solutions to some of these problems.

What is interesting is the author's ability to put these issues into a drama which the students of a rural new secondary school in Trinidad could handle competently.

The Ritual or
Friday Morning, First Period

Characters

Five 16-year-old schoolgirls, who take it in turns to play their
friend OMEGA, and who also act other characters as the action
proceeds. The girls are given numbers (1–5), and not names.
Teacher

Set

The classroom of a Senior Secondary School, on any Friday
morning. The students are on their own – a staff meeting is in
progress. Three tables (or desks) run from left to right across the
stage, a lectern is at far left. At far right is a stool, and there are
stools and chairs at various places. A blackboard stands at the
back. When the action begins all but the lectern, the blackboard
and the centre table are off stage. These are brought on by the
girls themselves as they come on from both sides.

    The girls all wear their school uniform. All changes in
character and personalities are done by the use of (a) small bits
of costume, a cap, pieces of white cloth (brought for needle-
work), aprons (brought for home economics) etc. (b) small
props (a two foot ruler becomes a baton, etc.) (c) the girls' own
acting.

Part 1

*The five girls come on slowly in a trance-like movement to symbolize the
concept of the ritual, to appropriate music. As the music stops the action
begins*

1: Joylyn goin' up for Queen show? But wha' jail is this?
2: So wha' wrong with that?

3: Wha' wrong with that? You think the people dem have they queen show for ugly people like Joylyn?

2: But how you could say she ugly? She have ah good figure.

1: Good figure? Good figure my foot. If Joylyn stand up straight she cyah see she big toe.

3: The gyul is 'bout 90-60-90.

4: And she eh talking metric.

5: Look in the first place she too black. Queen is for fair-skin people…and ah doh mean red-niggers.

2: All you have ah heart nah. If the gyul feel she good-looking, she good-looking. What you woulda do if you did born ugly like she?

3: To begin with I find she should leave the people queen show alone.

4: Wait till she taxi man find out.

5: Who, Joey? He go be glad. The chick go be a star. See she riding round in the PX taking loud marks.

1 (*imitating a master of ceremonies*): Ladies and gentlemen, presenting contestant number one, yet another Janelle 'Penny' Commisiong, Miss Everybody's Senior Secondary – Joylyn Francis.

ALL: Ray! Boo! Ray!

4: All yuh laugh – the next thing you know she win the show and gone up in the cold and leave all ah we down here.

3: Like you taking she serious o'wha?

5: Joylyn want one good man to cool she down, leh she behave she self.

3: Take care she doh get yours.

5: Wha'? She could take my man?

4: Why not? You eh have no use for him.

5: You know I eh have no use for him. You marking me or what?

4: Aright. Aright.

2: Ah hear Omega pregnant.

1: Who say so?

2: Doh ask me who say so.

1: Ah want to know, who say so?

2: No. You too fast.

1: A-A

2: I eh telling all yuh. All ah know is true. (No. 3 *sucks her teeth in disgust*) When all yuh do all yuh thing in the dark, what all yuh expect?

3: Me, sweetheart?

2: You go get your share.

3: Get my share? You think I is them stupid gyul or what?

2: So what happen, you cyah get pregnant?

3: Me chile. I too old in the business.

2: That's not the point. What you go do if you get pregnant?

3: Ah tell you, ah have more sense than that.

4: What happen, you is a dolly.

1: If you get pregnant what you go do?

2: Now as you in school?

4: With exams next year?

5: And yuh mother go want to kill you.

3: Throw it way nah, what you expect?

2: Not me.

1: Not you, and miss the carnival next year because yuh belly too big?

2: Not me.

3: You mean you go throw way the chance to go disco every weekend because yuh belly too big?

2: Um hmm.

4: You mean you go stay home from school and miss all this bachannal because yuh belly too big?

2: Um hmm. Not me. No.

1: No! She serious?

4: Wha' is this?

5: You going to eh play no basketball and netball for all dem months because yuh belly too big?

2: Um hmm.

1: You mean you go miss the chance to try ah lil wig-ah-licks every now and then with Ralphy because yuh belly too big?

2 (*convinced at last*): Well, as you say it so, ah could throw it way.

1: Or huh.

3: That's what ah saying.

4: Ah want to know.

2: Ah bet you Omega throwing way she own –

5: For she man to kill she. Rasta doh throw way child.

1: And she mother go kill she if she find out.

2: Eh eh. For what?

5: You doh know Omega mother.

3: Ah sure she keeping it.

2: Ah sure she throwing it way.

5: If you was Omega, what you woulda do?

3: Me. I is Omega?

5: No fool, But if you was Omega, you stupid eh.

3: But I is not Omega. Check Omega.

4: O God, the gyul is ah ass, yes. Play you is Omega.

5: Yes, pretend.

4: Just for ah lil while.

2: You is Omega. You does talk so much. What you woulda do?

3: Me?

2: Yes, you.

4: What you saying?

5: She only have mout'.

4: Say something daughter.

2: Suppose was you—

3: In serious?

ALL: In serious.

3: No joke?

ALL: No joke.

3: If was me I would throw…it…way.

Change of scene and personalities. No. 3 *becomes* OMEGA *while* No. 1 *becomes her boyfriend.*

1: No. I want the child. What you intend to do?

3: Hmm.

1: Omega, that eh really no answer. I really want to know what you doing.

3: What you want me to do?

1: Is one thing. I doh want you to kill it.

3: But if ah doh do that me mother go find out.

1: Why you worrying about your mother? This is between I and you.

3: How it could be between me and you? You forget I living
    home.

1: Well then, go and tell she.

3: You eh know my mother. Tell she she daughter pregnant
    for…ah…ah…Rastaman. You must be want the woman to
    dead.

1: Wha! You studyin' wha' people go say?

3: Michael, is not what people go say alone. I is 16; and you is 24.
    I going to school; you eh working no way. I pregnant…and
    you…you is ah Rasta.

1: True. I is Rasta. And I could stand I responsibilities.

3 (*sarcastically*): Yeh Jah go mind it.

1 (*missing the sarcasm*): Yeh. Jah go help I to educate I child;
    because wha', Jah give I life and you want to destroy it.

3: Michael, I wonder if you know what you talking 'bout. Is
    whether I keep the child for you or I throw it way. And the
    way I seeing it is best I get rid of…

1: Jah Rastafari, I, plant that seed in you for a reason him alone
    know. You might be destroying a future warrior, a king, a
    leader of the race.

3: Michael, you see all this stupidness.

1: Stupidness; you doubt the works of the Lion of Judah who
    alone know why he put that seed in your fertile soil…who
    knows what plans he have for you and the Black race?

3: Michael!

1: You cyah blow breath and you cyah give life, so why you
    should want to take another?

3: Look is I to catch, yes. So me eh able with this talk.

1: Woman let the child come forth and leave this Babylon
    wickedness alone.

3: But Michael, you eh trying to see my side.

1: Look; you hear what you say, is either you keep it or you kill it.
    You letting my life live? Yes or No?

3 pauses, then shakes her head.

1: Well is only one thing I have to say. If you kill my child you
    destroying my life and I really cyah deal with no woman
    who destroying I.

3: But Michael…Michael…Listen. Michael.

Return to the personalities of the schoolgirls.

4: Ai, come out ah that. Like you taking this thing serious or
   what?

2: Is only play you was playing, you know.

4: A-A. Like the gyul really crying for true yes.

5: If you had a man and he leave you, you go dead!

3: You know me eh have no man.

5: Ah only saying if…If…

3: What you bring for lunch?

5: Dead, you eh go want.

3: Why?

5 (*obviously teasing her*): You is ah Rasta gyul, you eh go eat
   chicken.

3: Was only play ah was playing, don' try that.

5: We go eat it lunch time. Wait.

3: You mightn't live till lunchtime. Leh we eat it now.

5: This gyul greedy eh.

3: Me eh eat this morning, you know.

5: Neither me.

2: You do the Spanish?

1: Me, you mad. And she better doh come and tell me nothing
   'bout no vocabulary. She have to humble.

4: A-A But hear this one. What is this m'lord!

5: M'lord! She say that just like Omega mother.

1: When Omega mother find out she pregnant, look ole mas'.

3: How she go find out? Omega throwing way the child.

1: That is what she tell Michael. But she bound to tell she
   mother.

5: And you go hear she mother. 'Omega, you what, pregnant?
   You mad. Out ah the house m'lord.'

1: She eh go say that man. Hear she: 'Omega, this is what I send
   you to school for? M'lord. Look at my trouble. You want to
   kill me o'what?'

4: 'O'what?' You feel Omega mother is ah soul gyul.

3: Well you tell me.

4: Let me show all you. When Omega mother get the news so,
　　she go stand up straight, watch Omega, put she hand on she
　　waist and say 'What it is you saying, m'lord?'

The personalities of OMEGA *and her* MOTHER *and later of her father now
emerge. No. 2 becomes* OMEGA *as No. 4 takes on the role of her* MOTHER.

OMEGA: Hmm. I don't know what I tell you for.

MOTHER: You right to say that, cause I don't know what the hell
　　I go do.

OMEGA: If daddy was here…

MOTHER: 'If your father was here'. Is he who have me in this
　　position. He never had time. Always all over the blasted
　　place.

OMEGA: O God Ma, doh start that again, doh start that again.
　　(*To audience*.) Eh, you tell me what I going to do. She saying
　　what she going to do. But you tell me what I going to do. 16
　　years and pregnant. And with a mother who doh under-
　　stand and who eh trying to understand. And…and with
　　really no father. It sounding strange, eh? But look. See what
　　I mean. It happening since ah small.

The MOTHER *becomes the* FATHER.

MOTHER AS FATHER: You better ask your mother, yes. Me eh
　　have
　　time for that now.

OMEGA (*at 10 yrs*): But Ma say to ask you.

MOTHER AS FATHER: You blasted mother always sending you to
　　me as if you is a boy child. Hmm. Which part this thing
　　taking place?

OMEGA (*at 10 yrs*): In school…ah could go?

MOTHER AS FATHER: Look, tell your mother, yes. I eh able.

OMEGA (*at 16 yrs again, and to the audience*): You see what ah
　　mean…just for me to go to ah lil class party, hear he. Now
　　hear she. (*At 10 yrs again*) Ma we having ah class party in
　　school Saturday and miss say…

MOTHER: Miss say, miss say. You see as you start coming with
　　'Miss say', go and ask your father.

OMEGA (*at 10 yrs*): But Ma…

MOTHER: Ah say to go and ask your father. He self never have time for me, much less for you. How much money you want for the party?

OMEGA (*at 10 yrs*): Ma, about two dollars to go in and…

MOTHER: Two dollars! Ask your father for true, yes.

OMEGA (*at 10 yrs*): If he give me ah could go…eh Ma…eh Ma?

MOTHER: Yes. Yes. Go.

OMEGA (*at 10 yrs*): Daddy, Ma say to give me two dollars to…

MOTHER AS FATHER: Your mother feel I making money or I is the Governer-General?

OMEGA (*at 10 yrs*): But she say how…

MOTHER AS FATHER: She could say what she feel to say, yes. Money doh come here by magic. Tell she that.

OMEGA (*at 10 yrs*): You better tell she for yourself.

MOTHER AS FATHER: What you say? Eh Omega? Bring your little tail here. You getting beside yourself. Eh. Ah bet ah box you in your mouth and make you swallow all your teeth. Eh, you little wretch.

OMEGA AS MOTHER: Rupert. Rupert. Doh hit me. You going mad.

MOTHER AS FATHER: You bitch. You take me for a damn fool or some little boy.

OMEGA AS MOTHER: You hit me again, you going to find out.

MOTHER AS FATHER: What you going to do, eh? Eh Merle? Go back to your mother as you accustom. Or run by Richard?

OMEGA AS MOTHER: O God, Rupert, not that again. You still with this stupidness. I eh see the damn man in months. You eh have no shame. You want your daughter to hear you. Talk hard. Let Omega hear. Let all the neighbours hear. Let everybody hear. What kind of house is this, m'lord!

MOTHER AS FATHER: Sometimes I does feel to bus' your blasted face.

OMEGA AS MOTHER: Rupert, not in front of the child.

MOTHER AS FATHER: Look, the quicker I get out ah this place…

OMEGA AS MOTHER: O God Rupert, again. Omega now going to write the Common Entrance you bringing up this nonsense about going away again.

MOTHER AS FATHER: Ah tell you already. Merle, ah going to make ah living for you and the child.

OMEGA AS MOTHER: Me, Rupert? Me? To mind me m'lord? (*She*

reverts to the personality of OMEGA.) For what? Nobody eh care
'bout me. (*To audience*.) Ent you see that. You see and hear
for yourself. Mother plus father plus daughter equal
confusion with ah capital C.

OMEGA *and* MOTHER *speak alternatingly until* OMEGA *is left to continue
alone.*

OMEGA: So when I ask what I go do, you understand my
    situation.

MOTHER: How I could ever understand this? My own daughter
    who for the last how much years I minding without a father,
    who I selling and sinning my soul for.

OMEGA: After all. Ah mean what you expect? I come from a poor
    family, father gone away; mother struggling to survive or
    surviving to struggle. Same thing.

MOTHER: Look at you Omega, look at you. 16 years and making
    child.

OMEGA: I getting up half-past four, five o'clock in the morning to
    go to school. Time I reach they I tired like hell. And you
    know them Senior Sec. School. Well that is chaos self, ole
    mas! No teacher half the time. And it so big it like the whole
    ah Port-of-Spain, ah concrete jungle self.

MOTHER: Tell me what you going to do? Throw way the child;
    keep it; stay home; go and live with the child father; start to
    whore; drown yourself. Eh! What to do?

OMEGA: So I skip school now and then and go down the road and
    lime. That is ah crime, eh? I eh thief and I eh kill. Yet. You
    think it easy?

MOTHER: The same thing ah did tell your father, before he leave –
    'doh send she to that new Junior Sec. School; doh send she
    to that new Junior Sec. School'. Ah tell him, you hear, Lord
    knows, ah tell him.

OMEGA: Sometimes when I get up lil' late and have time to eat
    something, when it have something, that is, I does be so
    hungry by the time recess, that is best I stay out the road
    and lime – at least ah could get something to full meh belly.

MOTHER: Ah say 'Rupert, let she take over the exams. Let she
    take it over. Or go and see the minister see if you could get

ah transfer to one ah them good schools.' Ah tell him.

OMEGA: All you could laugh, yes, you doh know what it is to be hungry and fed up. You went to ah good school. You sure you woulda pass exam and get work. Most ah all you used to study on ah full stomach or you had so much false pride you used to believe it full. Well I get stick and my belly fulling. So what? After the first time it does be easy; you have nothing to lose, if you know what I mean.

MOTHER: Ah tell him. All them little women in them school is whore. But he wouldn' listen.

OMEGA: Take me, for instance – not literally please, – ah had enough ah that. (*She speaks these last lines with* No. 5 *who becomes the next* OMEGA.) But look at my situation. After all I tell you – too often hungry, frustrated and fed-up ah school and what eh go happen when ah leave. So ah reach to school one day and stop to lime on the road.

Actresses all change to personalities in a court room. No. 1 *is* DEFENCE LAWYER; No. 2, *a* CLERK *in the court;* No. 3, *the* JUDGE; No. 4, STATE LAWYER; No. 5 *takes the role of* OMEGA *for this scene.*

STATE: Your Honour, I fail to see the relevance of all this.

JUDGE: Yes. Yes. Counsel for Defence?

DEF: Your Honour, if I am permitted the defendant's personal life is of the utmost importance to the case.

JUDGE: Yes. Yes. But she is not charged with failing to go to school or with any conflict she might have had with the socio-political system.

DEF: Certainly Sir, Defence is aware of this. But it is our belief that a knowledge of her background will throw considerable light…

JUDGE: Does Counsel intend to use the defendant's past as a form of defence? Certainly the law does not permit…

DEF: I am quite aware, Your Honour, but if I may be allowed to continue for a while longer with this line of questioning, I am sure that I can show…

JUDGE: Yes. Yes. You had better. State Counsel?

STATE: Agreed, Your Honour, provided that Defence gets to the point.

DEF: Now Omega, tell the court why you came…eh…why you
    did what you did.

OMEGA: Well ah was fed-up…of school…of home…of every
    damn thing.

DEF: Go on.

OMEGA: And then I meet Michael.

DEF: That is Michael Hackett, Your Honour, her former…

OMEGA: Boyfriend.

DEF: Yes, tell us of your first meeting. Start from the very
    beginning.

OMEGA: I remember the first time I meet Michael. Me and
    Joylyn gone down by she grandmother for lunch. This time
    we leave school about 10 o'clock so and we gone up the
    road. When we reach round by the parlour – ah lil green
    shop that does sell bread alone – yeh, well that is all I does
    see on the counter. It have ah track to go through to come
    out on the road where she grandmother living. As we reach
    out the road ah see this Rastaman sitting down on the side.
    The man have one long dread and it jet black. Ai. Well
    I…you know…Since then every time I see him he only
    watching me and eh saying nothing. Well me eh saying
    nothing neither. Until one day I alone coming from by
    Joylyn – that was the day she mother come back from
    Canada. Ah passing through the track, me eh even
    studying he, all of sudden ah hear ah voice say, 'Sister,
    where your friend? Like she sick o'what?' Well ah didn't
    know what to say. Ah say 'nah, she eh going to school
    today'. Since then we start to talk.

She does the following dialogue between herself and MICHAEL, *operating
as both characters.*

MICHAEL: What you doing Saturday, Omega?

OMEGA: Staying home.

MICHAEL: Step my side.

OMEGA: Me?

MICHAEL: Like you doh trust I o'what? It having a dub out by
    Stevie.

OMEGA: Nah. How I going home after? If Joylyn was going, but she have to go for practice for the queen show.

MICHAEL: So what? You go reach home.

OMEGA: I eh know. If you hear my mother find out I does be
liming down here, much less to go party. You mad.

She continues her story.

OMEGA: But you know yuh gyul did bound to end up in the lil'
something. Ah tell me mother how ah going to spend the
night by Joylyn. And was true, because me and Joylyn end
up in the party. But me eh see she for the night, I and
Michael and some other Rasta lime ah lil' way outside the
party. Them smoking they kaya and thing.

JUDGE: Their what?

DEF: Kaya – a slang for marijuana, M'lord.

JUDGE: Oh.

DEF: Of course, you yourself did not and never did partake of the
stuff?

OMEGA: No, Sir.

DEF: Have you ever had sexual intercourse with Michael?

OMEGA *looks pleadingly at the* JUDGE.

JUDGE: Answer the question.

OMEGA *nods*.

DEF: Have you ever had sexual intercourse with anyone before
Michael?

OMEGA *shakes her head*.

DEF: I know this is going to hurt, but I'll try to make it as easy for
you as possible. I want you to answer truthfully. Remember
you are under oath. Have you ever had sexual relations
with anyone other than Michael?

OMEGA: Of course not. What kind of girl do you think I am?

DEF: And these ridiculous charges are certainly not true.

OMEGA: No.

DEF: No further questions, Your Honour.

STATE: Just one or two questions, M'lord. You have told the
court that you were actually 'liming outside a party'.

OMEGA: Yes.

STATE: And that you were there in the company of some young
men, among whom was one Michael Hackett, your

sweetheart, who deserted you the moment you became pregnant?

OMEGA: He did not. He left because…

STATE: Because you were pregnant.

OMEGA: He did not. Sir?

STATE: O.K. Be that as it may. Were you in the habit of sleeping with him?

OMEGA: Your Honour!!

STATE: M'lord, the defendant is charged with a serious crime and defence is claiming that the accused has never had sexual relations with anyone but her so-called boyfriend, and therefore was not capable of…

DEF (*objecting*): My lord!

JUDGE: Yes. Yes.

STATE: Let me put it another way. You claim to be an innocent schoolgirl whose only knowledge of sex is with a so-called Rastafarian and you know nothing of the charge for which you now face the court.

OMEGA: Yes.

STATE: And you expect the court to believe that you, a girl, were standing in the darkened street at two in the morning, all alone, because the friends you were with ran from the scene?

OMEGA: Your Honour!

STATE: Just answer the question 'Yes' or 'No'.

JUDGE: I'm afraid you'll have to.

OMEGA: I…

STATE: Yes or no?

OMEGA: Yes. So what? That is ah crime?

STATE: So you were no easy-to-fool virgin when you were arrested that night for…

OMEGA: Your Honour.

JUDGE: Calm down and answer.

OMEGA (*shouting*): No. No.

JUDGE: If you persist in these outbursts I'll have you removed from the court until…

OMEGA (*trying to control herself*): O.K. O.K.

STATE: How many other men have you slept with?

OMEGA: Your Honour!

JUDGE (*upholding the objection*): Yes.

STATE: Your only intention in stopping Constable Jerimiah was to get a lift home?

OMEGA: Yes.

STATE: And your so-called boyfriend. He also ran, leaving you all alone in the middle of the night?

OMEGA: He went to check out a drop.

STATE: So that when the car approached, not recognizing the officer, you were quite willing to 'check out a drop?'

OMEGA: No. I…

STATE: I put it to you that when Constable Jerimiah picked you up that night, that was exactly what it was – a pick up, not for him but for you.

OMEGA (*reverting during this outburst to her real schoolgirl self*): No. What the hell you think. I explain to you what I was doing. Too besides me eh playing again, damit. I eh playing.

They all revert to their school personalities.

1: How you mean you eh playing?

4: Look, let we finish the thing, nah.

5: I cyah take much more ah this nah.

4: So what? Let we done it. Me eh go feel good until we come to the end.

5: No.

1 (*angrily*): No, my ass. You know damn well why we doing it and we going to do it.

5: What it going to prove eh! What it going to prove?

1: It going to prove what it have to because all ah we is Omega. You and you and you; all ah we. All woman who ever love before or get love before; or skip school or storm taxi or cuss teacher or screw after party, all is Omega. And all ah we who carry the guilt of a girl who get pregnant but didn't want to get pregnant. So we going to become Omega for a little while to understand she feelings, to know she better, to understand she better, cause is like to know we better.

5: Me eh feeling nothing. I just feeling like ah ass.

1: Regardless, we go try.

5: Look how much thing Omega do, you eh want we to do all that?

2: Ah want to know.

5: Remember how she cuss that stupid English teacher.

2: And she skip school and went by the beach the other day.

1: Hush!

2: And she help tief from the snackette.

5: And remember the time she…

1 (*slapping her*): Ah say we doing it and we damn well doing it, if we have to do a thousand scenes, play a thousand plays, perform a thousand rituals until we understand Omega – not Omega the end – but Omega the beginning of a New Society. Is 400 years now we playing Omega. Like is since forever we is Omega. Since we step off them slave ships Caribbean Woman is Omega, hustling man and getting seeded. Never sure who the father is. Like rabbit, we making child every year. Making we mothers grand-mothers at 35, making a mockery of womanhood and an affair of sex. So we go try, we go become Omega until we understand and come so strong that Caribbean woman cyah get exploited again. Until Black woman could walk tall with they heads held high. Cause if we cyah see that day even in we minds, then there is no hope. NOT NOW; NOT EVER.

They immediately stop acting and return to their trance-like state as in the beginning, with the music in the back-ground until they are ready for Part 2.

END OF PART 1

Part 2

Part 2 begins where Part 1 left off, when OMEGA *stopped 'playing'.*

2: Try it nah.

1: O God, look how far we reach.

5: Aright, but if she ask me anymore shit I done eh.

4: O.K. What you want me to ask you?

5: Just doh ask me no more shit.

They all change to their court personalities.

JUDGE: If Defence Counsel would like a short recess…

DEF: Omega?

OMEGA: Is all right.

STATE: So that after such a far-fetched story, you expect us to believe that a young woman who has been living with how many Rastafarian…

OMEGA: You see, Your Honour, you see.

JUDGE: I am afraid…

OMEGA: I doh care what the hell you 'fraid. I going.

JUDGE: But…

OMEGA: But nothing. Let me pass. I going, man, I going. Move.

JUDGE: Remove the accused.

OMEGA (*struggling with the* CLERK): Leggo me!

JUDGE: Remove the accused from the docks.

OMEGA: Leave me. Ah going to kill one ah all you.

JUDGE: Get the prisoner out of here.

OMEGA: I is ah fool eh.

JUDGE: Get out of my court. Get out of here. (*The* JUDGE *changes into an angry* SHOPKEEPER.) Get to hell out of here.

All characters change. In the three short scenes that follow, No. 3 and No. 2 become the SHOPKEEPER *and the* LADY PASSER-BY *of scene 1, while No. 1 plays* OMEGA. *In scene 2, No. 5 is the* FEMALE PASSENGER, *No. 1 is the* TAXI-DRIVER, *while No. 4 is* OMEGA. *In the third scene, No. 4 and No. 2 are the* FIRST *and* SECOND WORKER/limer *respectively, and No. 3 plays* OMEGA. *As No. 1 had demanded earlier on, they are all going to become* OMEGA *for a little while until they understand her better.*

Scene 1

SHOPKEEPER: All you blasted young people is too much damn thief. Ah doh want all you in me shop again. Too damn thief.

OMEGA: You doh know what ah want to thief?

LADY: Mister, what they take?

SHOPKEEPER: What they take. They eh get nothing this time. But if ah get meh hands on them…the bitches.

LADY: They from the Senior Sec.?

SHOPKEEPER: Senior Sec.? I doh know why the government wasting money on these good-for-nothing…all over the place looking for what ah doh know.

LADY: Mister you musn't say that.

SHOPKEEPER: Eh-heh…If I tell you something. A young girl come in me store the other morning, say she come for…

Scene 2

OMEGA (*trying the hitch a ride*): Oropouche Junction? Haul you mudder…

PASSENGER: How these girls always out ah the school so, all hour ah the day?

TAXI-DRIVER: Girls? Them is little women, yes.

PASSENGER: They must be from the evening shift?

TAXI-DRIVER: Nah. Dem school eh have no shift.

PASSENGER: Then why…

TAXI-DRIVER: They know what they looking for.

PASSENGER: Some of these parents should see….

TAXI-DRIVER: Madam, dem is big woman, yes. Ha ya yai. If ah tell you ah story. Two to three ah them come in the car the other day. Ah pick them up by Oropouche Junction. Was when? Monday? What today is…yes…Monday…

Scene 3

1ST WORKER: Niceness, say something, nah.

OMEGA: Wha', you want something o'what?

1ST WORKER: A-A. But how you hot so?

OMEGA: Hotness make me.

2ND WORKER: Leave the gyul, nah. You ent see she eh want you.

1ST WORKER: She eh want me. She want ah good…

OMEGA: You know what I want?

2ND WORKER (*to* OMEGA): Sweetheart, why you doh go to school? (*Offering her a cigarette.*) Heh, smoke something and cool yourself. What happen, you eh want it?

Return to their school personalities.

3: Nah, in class? you mad?
2: Wha' you 'fraid?
4: Look I tired yes.
1: Tired do what?
4: Whole morning all you carrying on as if you eh human. Look
   how all you have the classroom.
1: So what? We go fix it back.
2: You want ah smoke?
1: Nah, it go smell.
2: Doh dig, it eh have no class in the next room.
3: Suppose ah teacher pass.
5: When saying so, where them teachers?
2: It having ah staff meeting.
5: No wander Babbsy eh reach yet. I say she stay home.
2: Babbsy could ever stay home.
5: All you smoking the thing or not?
1: Not me. Me eh getting in no trouble for all you.
5: You done in trouble already.
1: Me? All you. Me eh give Omega...
2: Hush...
5: All you smoking or what?
1: Not me.
3: Me neither.
5: All you is weakheart or what?
3: You could say what you want, yes.
2: Well, go by the door in case.

No. 3 *and* No. 1 *go to the door.*

5 (*referring to the cigarette*): Light it.

No.2 *lights it and begins to smoke.*

5: What happen? You go take all?
2: Wait nah.
5: 2 drag. Is only one, you know.
2: Ah could take in some rockers now.

5: Yes I.

2: How?

5: Wait nah. First period eh done yet?

2: Nah, but the bell go ring just now.

5 (*singing*): Love is all I bring, in meh khaki suit and ting.

2: Run the collie, yes I.

Character change: No. 2, RASTA BROTHER; No. 5, MICHAEL, OMEGA's *boyfriend*. No. 4 *becomes the next* OMEGA.

RASTA: Where you get this? By wire o' what?

MICHAEL: Nah. Ah brother from down by Freddie side bring down some Columbian.

RASTA: What I. The real stuff.

MICHAEL: How.

RASTA: What happen fus' night up by you, king? The man hear the Babby step up so with loud car and thing?

MICHAEL: Seen.

RASTA: Man get make up, sah.

MICHAEL: Seen.

RASTA: These men is wickedness, yes Dread.

MICHAEL: Man say is Dread-I who bring the Babby. I sight him up in the jungle this morning.

RASTA: Yes. But I still stay with love for the brother. Yes king. I is true Rasta. As long as I have the guidance of I God, Haile I, Selassie I, no evil could overcome I.

OMEGA: These men is wicked-ness yes.

RASTA: Yesterday sah, the man stepping round by I step-buck side. I with a loud piece ah kaya. Yes I. As ah step so by the region to go in by Stevie, who could bounce up I but the king Babby.

MICHAEL: Randy?

RASTA: He self sah.

MICHAEL: Wha' you do?

RASTA: Well, the man stop the car and watching I in ah form. I study if he only movements towards I, I plan to scant, yes, I.

OMEGA: What happen?

RASTA: Well you know how the Dread stay righteous in the face

of the weakheart and them. I stare him straight in he face
and the man start the car and forward. How.

MICHAEL: I hear your friend fighting the Babylon cattle market.

OMEGA: Who? Joylyn?

MICHAEL: Yeh, she going for queen show.

OMEGA: She know what she doing; that is what she want.

MICHAEL: I know you overs that.

OMEGA: True.

RASTA: Haile, I stepping yes.

MICHAEL: More times, Dread.

Enter two policemen – the two girls, Nos. 1 *and* 3, *who were at the door.*
No. 1 *is the* SARGEANT, No. 3 *the* CONSTABLE.

SARGEANT: Stay right they. Stay right they.

RASTA: Ai. Not me Babby.

CONSTABLE: Stand up they. Like this one have something,
Sarge.

RASTA: Not I.

CONSTABLE: Not I? Turn round. You. Turn round.

SARGEANT: You too. Turn round and kneel down.

CONSTABLE: Down.

SARGEANT: I eh want no Rasta in this country. None. You!
(*addressing* OMEGA) What you doing here?

OMEGA: Me?

SARGEANT: Yes, you. Who the hell you think I talking to?

OMEGA: I…

MICHAEL: Man, that is meh sister. She just come up to
check…

SARGEANT? That is your sister. What she doing here this hour ah
the night?

MICHAEL: She come up to ah party.

CONSTABLE: Come up to ah party, eh!

SARGEANT: Constable, take she name and let she go. And miss,
the next time I hear or I catch you in anything, you going
down. You hear that.

CONSTABLE: We carrying them down, Sarge?

SARGEANT: Look, ah giving all you ah chance. Doh let me find
you on the street again.

RASTA: I know you eh like Rasta.

SARGEANT: And hush, before I finish you off. Come, Constable.

They both leave.

OMEGA: Michael.
MICHAEL: Yes.
OMEGA: I want to go home.
MICHAEL: Alright. I going and see if I could organize some
     transport. Wait here.
OMEGA: Me alone?
MICHAEL: Sight. But doh worry, ah just checking by the 'dub'.
OMEGA: Alright, but do quick.
END OF PART 2

MICHAEL *leaves and Part 3 is about to begin. Appropriate background music should be used.* No. 1 *from by the door turns and speaks.*

Part 3

1: Alright, the last ritual, the very best. One more.

No. 4 *is an* ELDER *of an African Community;* No. 3, NNEKA, *African woman;* No. 2, SON OF ELDER; No. 1, ONIKA (OMEGA), *daughter of* NNEKA; *and* No. 5 *is an* ATTENDANT *to the* ELDER.

ELDER: Rise, my son, and let us hear this good news which you
     are so eager to tell.
SON: The news is both good and bad, my father.
ELDER: Good and bad? Explain, my son.
SON: Onika, my father, the only daughter of Nneka, is with
     child, my child, and...
ELDER: And you are not yet married. I see. You need not worry.
     Even the gods are human sometimes. They will under-
     stand. Bring Onika to me and let us together give thanks to
     Oya, goddess of fertility, for this great favour she has
     bestowed upon us.
SON: She waits outside, my father.
ELDER: Let her approach.

At No. 2's *signal* Nos. 1 *and* 3 *approach.*

ELDER: Welcome Nneka, wife of Maduke, great warrior, now
 returned to our ancestors.

NNEKA: I am honoured, my lord.

ELDER: Greetings Onika, daughter of Nneka, let not the fact that
 you are not yet married deter you from rejoicing. (*He claps to*
 summon the ATTENDANT.) Call Adunna, oldest and wisest of
 all our priests and let us give thanks and praise to Oya. (*The*
 ATTENDANT *leaves. He turns to* ONIKA.) For through you and
 this child yet to be born our people can experience not only
 the past but the present and the future to come. Let Adunna
 come and we shall perform the ritual of pregnancy that has
 been ours and will be ours forever.

The drums sound for a few seconds before they all come out of their
play-acting.

1: That was good, eh Omega? (*speaking naturally to any and all of*
 them since they have all experienced OMEGA – *Caribbean Woman.*)

2: Yeh, what you saying Omega?

4: True. That was really good.

They are all relaxed as if a great burden has been lifted.

5: All you, Miss coming.

They hastily arrange the tables and chairs in a proper manner and sit
awaiting the arrival of the TEACHER.

TEACHER: What is going on here? Leave you all alone for a
 minute and you want to disturb the entire school. You all
 have no work to do?

2: No, Miss.

TEACHER: 'No, Miss'?

2 AND 5: Yes, Miss.

TEACHER: Well do something. Every teacher has a complaint
 about this class. When it is not talking it is walking about
 the school. When it is not that it is something else. You all

ever sit down and think about your future? We had a staff meeting this morning. You know to discuss what? A schoolgirl; from this school. Yes; The police had to lock her up early this morning, late last night for prostitution. One of your fellow students. If you all didn't have such a poor reputation, you think this could have happened? All hour of the day when you suppose to be in school, you knocking about the place.

1: Me, Miss?

TEACHER: Yes, you Miss Innocent. When you all not down in the junction harrassing the people in the shops, you are interfering with the people on the road.

1: Miss, them does interfere with we first.

TEACHER: And the poor taxi-drivers!

4: Miss, she still in jail?

TEACHER: Of course not. But think of the embarrassment to the school. You all don't think of the school? And she might even have to stand trial (No. 1 *sniggers*.) Yes, laugh. It could have been anyone of you. You all should be ashamed and just as guilty. All of this happening to a fellow student of yours and you sit here talking nonsense and being idle. Don't take your school work more seriously and see if you don't end up like her. Furthermore I want your names for future reference. Stand and give your names.

They stand and give their real names, for the first time, as the curtain falls.

CURTAIN

Textual notes

page

53   Omega: the final letter of the Greek alphabet, signifying 'the end, the final, the ultimate'.

54   queen show: Carnival Queen competition, which is partly a beauty contest.

54   Penny: Janelle 'Penny' Commisiong, a former Trinidad beauty queen who went on to win the 'Miss Universe' title.

55   bacchanal: (here) the little day-to-day 'scandals' of school life.

57   Most of the Rasta talk is roughly international Rasta 'language'. A director should try to be accurate and avoid taking liberties as the writer has been quite painstaking.

       Jah: God (Haile Selassie I of Ethiopia).

       Lion of Judah: one of the titles of Haile Selaissie I.

       cyah: can't.

       is I to catch: I am the one in trouble.

       Babylon: Rasta talk for the *status quo*; western society.

58   dead: cooked meat; the flesh of a dead animal.

61   You think it easy?: 'it' here means 'life'.

63   dread: the hairstyle of the Rastafari, also called 'locks' or 'dreadlocks'.

64   lime/liming outside a party: standing outside the premises where the party is held, conversing and enjoying the music.

66   storm: gatecrash, (here) ride without paying.

70   doh dig: don't 'dig' anything – don't be scared or concerned.

70–1 rockers: reggae music.

       'Love is all I bring': a line from 'Three Piece Suit', a popular reggae number.

       collie: marijuana.

       fus' night: first night, meaning last night (Rasta slang).

       Babby: Babylon, (here) the police.

       loud car: police car with siren.

       make up: locked up.

71–2 jungle: concrete jungle – an urban low-income housing
       area.
    loud piece ah kaya: a sizeable amount of high-quality
       marijuana.
    king Babby: a prominent policeman.
    In ah form: not directly, surreptitiously.
    movements: makes a move.
    to scant: to become scarce, to flee.
    fighting the cattle market: entering a beauty competition.
    overs that: dismiss that, are bigger than that and will
       ignore it.
    more times: till another time.
73 dub: reggae party.

Questions for the class or cast

Some of these questions are directed mainly to players, but all
are useful for general discussion.

1. Why is the play called *The Ritual*? Why is the ritual element
   important to an understanding of what the play is about?
2. Why is there not a full 'set' on stage?
3. Why do the girls all play Omega at one point or another?
4. Why do they all play other parts as well?
5. The play begins with the girls talking about Joylyn's entry
   in the 'queen show'. Near the end, reference is made to the
   show as 'Babylon cattle market'. Discuss the difference
   (and the reasons for the difference) in the girls' attitudes to
   the show at these two points in the play.
6. The play seems to be dealing with more than the reasons for
   and problems of schoolgirl pregnancy. What else does it
   deal with? What issues does the author think are the more
   fundamental?
7. At the end of the play the teacher makes three statements:
   (a) 'She might even have to stand trial', (b) 'It could have
   been any one of you'; (c) 'Think about your future'.

What is the significance of each of these statements and of the teacher's position in general?

8. Why are: (a) the names of the girls only given at the end? (b) The actresses real names given?
9. Why is the 'last' ritual described as the 'best'?
10. What is the author saying about the attitude of the traditional African society to pregnancy and birth? What is the significance of this?
11. What differences and similarities does one see in the attitudes of the police when compared to that of the teacher?
12. None of the adults in the play relates positively or in an understanding manner to the girls. (a) What is the significance of this? (b) What are the reasons for this?
13. Would you say that the school has been negligent? Why?

Some further questions

These questions are more specific. Some are directed to the teacher–director (e.g. questions 9, 10) but again all are useful for general class discussion.

1. (*pages* 53–6) What are the main concerns of this group of girls at this stage in their lives?
2. (*pages* 56–7) Discuss the pros and cons of Michael's argument.
3. (*pages* 57–8) Why has No. 3 become so overwrought in her playacting?
4. (*pages* 57–8) Why does No. 1 not join in the teasing?
5. (*pages* 59–62) Discuss the relationships between: (a) Mother and Father; (b) both parents and Omega.
    How does an insight into these relationships help us to understand Omega?
6. (*pages* 61–2) The actor speaks directly to the audience here. (a) Why is this included at this point? (b) Does it weaken or strengthen the play?
7. (*pages* 62–3) The scene before (and those to come) has been a flash-back during a courtroom sequence. For what is Omega on trial? Can we also say that in this play it is the

court (or legal system, or even the society) that is on trial? If
so, for what? What would be your verdict?

8. (*pages* 66–7) Why is there conflict over finishing the scene?

9. (*pages* 66–7) No. 1 has gained tremendous insight. Is this
believable, or is this the device? That is, should an actress
play this moment simply as a girl in a class, or should the
actress and director have it played with 'something underlying', to show that she is more than a girl in a class?

10. (*page* 67) How is No. 1's speech an example of a moment
where the use of the ritual element can help to underline the
point and to move away from 'preachyness' and towards a
deeper kind of realism?

11. (*pages* 67–8) What is the underlying connection between
these scenes? What do they tell us about adult attitudes to
the searching, confused young persons of the 1980s?

12. (*pages* 68–9) Is Omega an innocent bystander, or an
integral 'knowing' part of the game/system/play?

13. (*page* 70) Where are the teachers? What is the significance of
their absence?

14. (*pages* 68–71) What is the 'mood' (and rhythm) of these
three mini-scenes? How do they contrast with the scene in
the classroom immediately following? (Note the brazen,
aggressive 'womanishness' of the role they play in public as
against the normal schoolgirl mischief of the classroom.)

15. (*pages* 72–3) What about speech and body rhythms in the
mini-scene here? How should they differ from other moments immediately before and after?

16. (*pages* 72–3) What really happened on the night of Omega's
arrest? Is any one person (or group of persons) at fault?

17. (*pages* 74–5) What are the ironies involved here?

Production notes

Two important and closely related features of the play are: the
writer's use of symbolism; and the ritual element which
underlies all of the action.

In a production which 'uses' this ritual element fully the symbolism can be further heightened. One should also note that there are moments in the dialogue when the lines may seem, at first glance, to be coming directly from the author. This, in a play of this nature, is not the weakness that it may be in other work. Often this omniscient (authorial) presence may be made into a strength by proper use of the ritual element.

Using the ritual

The director needs to decide on what he is to use to create the ritual feel or atmosphere. He can use as a base an actual Caribbean ritual – one that is relevant to the 'message' of the play. Elements from this ritual can be stylized and heightened for the purposes of the production. The director and cast can create their own ritual by giving significance to certain body positions, group formations, vocal and other sounds, etc. In either of the cases suggested, or while using any other method, accompanying music, sound or lighting effects can be introduced to give additional texture.

One needs to be careful, at the same time, not to create an atmosphere of unreality. In fact, anything that might suggest that what is being portrayed is unreal or a dream should be eschewed. The play deals strongly with reality, and in our day to day existence ritual is used to deal with those aspects of our lives that are very important or have deep symbolic significance. (Consider popular rituals: ceremonies of marriage, christening, burial and other religious rites, the Jewish Bar Mitzvah, the law courts, examination procedures, formal dinners etc.)

After you have decided on what is being used to create the ritual, and have established this early in the play, elements of it (or perhaps all of it) need to be repeated at carefully chosen intervals, to lend a unity to the production, to serve as a constant but subtle reminder, and to tie it all together clearly. A fairly obvious opportunity to do so lies in the moments during some of the 'scene changes' (those moments where the action shifts to another place or another time).

Set design

The set for this play should be a very flexible one. Scene changes should be effected with minimum effort and yet the stage picture for each scene should be different enough to create the feel of another setting.

The props and set can actually be more basic than the writer suggests. Five or six 'boxes' – 2 feet tall and 1½ feet square – can be the complete set. One may add a blackboard (placed at a position that does not dominate, but which can be brought into focus when needed) and a larger box–shape which can be a teacher's desk, a judge's table, etc. These two features are optional and should be dispensed with if they become at all problematic or clumsy.

The classroom setting presents a challenge to the director. He must avoid the flatness of one or two lines of desks, chairs, boxes, or whatever he chooses to use, stretched across the stage. At the same time any arrangement that lacks some symmetry will lose the 'classroom feel' as well as the opportunity to make a statement about the regimentation of the classroom.

A diagonal line can be very useful as it has scope for much variety in stage patterns. If for example the diagonal runs from downstage right to upstage left, observe the possible variations:

Basic set
(1)

by changing the position of boxes 4 and 5 one gets:

(2)

by moving boxes 2 and 4:

(3)

by moving boxes 1 and 2:

(4)

by moving boxes 1 and 4:

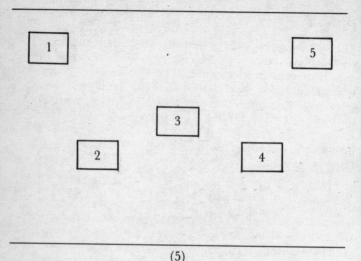

(5)

and a number of other patterns. A different stage picture can also be achieved by a change of direction in the persons sitting on the boxes (or a change of focus). These changes help to keep the action on the stage fluid and make the picture easier on the eye and more interesting.

One should remember that any movement of the set will be carried out by the cast and should be done in a stylized (but brisk) manner. It can be done in a way which enhances the ritual element of the play.

Some points to consider

The text/script

In producing the play for performance some teachers may want to alter a few of the 'stronger' words in the play. These can be changed as follows: 'whore' (page 61) to 'sell yourself' or 'prostitute'; 'screw' (page 66) to 'have sex'; 'ass' (page 66) to 'idiot'; 'shit' (page 67) to 'foolishness'.

Pacing

The play should be briskly paced. If it drags at all the whole rhythm and balance of the piece can be lost. The director has to use a ritual concept which will enhance this and allow the actors to aim at capturing the vivacity of a group of exuberant schoolgirls. Remember that the girls are bored and frustrated at the beginning of the class but they become progressively more involved during the course of the action. Their excitement (and involvement) grows as they investigate the reality of Omega/ Caribbean woman.

The play

The play is cathartic. The catharsis takes place on the stage with the student–players. The teacher is way behind the students (and the audience) by the end of the play. It is clear that the writer's intention is for the catharsis to affect the actors themselves – during the course of rehearsals – as well as the audience.

But the play is also didactic. Mr Constance wishes to explain to us his view of the situation/problem in which the Caribbean woman finds herself. He chooses to suggest a solution as well – and herein lies a problem for some persons. Although the 'African' scene works well dramatically, some persons may feel that it makes too weak, or too naive, or too incomplete a statement. But the problem has been interestingly and poignantly stated and therefore, intrinsic to the play-reading/ rehearsal process is the useful classroom, or 'director and cast' exercise – 'Wherein lies the solution?' Depending on the bent of the teacher/director and the class/cast the ensuing discussion could have a political, a sociological, or a religious base – or all of these.

3 *Good Morning Miss Millie*

by Aldwyn Bully

This is one of those good rural comedies that are so popular at festivals. The characters are thinly drawn but this does not detract as there is a great deal suggested in the script that actors and director can use to flesh them out into really workable parts.

In a swift-moving plot the main protagonist, Miss Millie, receives her late father's will in which she is bequeathed quite a lot of property and money on the condition that she gets married to a certain man – the son of a friend of her father's.

Miss Millie, in trying to satisfy the demands of the will, seems determined to make a number of terrible, if amusing, mistakes – and she almost succeeds. There are a number of clever twists in the plot which moves briskly to its denouement where everything is put right and all turns out happily.

The action is swift, the situations very amusing and the characters are believable. If enough gusto is put into it, this play will probably always work as well as it did in the 1981 Schools Drama Festival in Kingston, where Meadowbrook High School had so much fun with it.

Good Morning Miss Millie

A comedy in one act

Characters

MILLIE MAUPAS, a country woman of about 44
HELEN, her daughter, about 18
CELCUS ALECK WORKMAN, a young man of about 20
ALECK 'TAZ' WORKMAN, his father about 48
MARY
LIZZIE
ANNIE } friends of MILLIE
WALIX
JACK
MR LINKSON, a lawyer
A SMALL BOY
VILLAGERS

Set

Millie's home. The room is small, with numerous pictures,
calendars, etc. on the partitions. There is a door leading to the
village road up-stage centre, with windows on either side. The
door stage left leads to the kitchen, door stage right to a
bedroom. A number of chairs placed along the partitions and a
small table with framed photographs and a bouquet of artificial
flowers somewhat left of stage centre.

Scene 1: *As the play opens two candles burn on the small table as*
MILLIE, *her daughter* HELEN *and a small group of friends and relatives
kneel in a rough semicircle. They are all dressed in sombre colours on the
last night of prayers for Millie's father.*

PRAYER-LEADER: May the soul of thy servant John Joseph

Jeremiah Maupas and all the faithful departed through the mercy of God rest in peace....

ALL: Amen

They all cross themselves and stand, murmuring quietly to each other, most of them taking seats.

MILLIE (*going to blow out candles*): Helen, go in the kitchen and get the cups and the coffee for the guests and den when you finish look in de safe you'll see de wine an' a box of biscuits, bring dem too.

HELEN: Yes Ma. (*she goes out*)

MILLIE: Everybody comfortable? Good. I send Helen to get de few little things to put in the stomach, so have no fear. I so glad all-you could come and pray with me for old Papy.

MARY: Millie, you know it was our pleasure to come, Ol' Papy Maupas was such a nice, gentle man. An' you yourself Millie, you does be nice to everybody in the village, we couldn't let you down.

MILLIE: Thank you my dear.

MARY: But Papy Maupas was really a nice man you know. You remember de day when he was walking to town with de sheeps for him to sell in de market and de two sheeps get away an' run right back here. Papy run all de way back here behind dem, an' when he reach he say, since de sheeps dem didn't want to go to town he would sell dem right here. An' he slaughter dem dat same afternoon and sell de meat to the village. Boy, I had never eat so much pork before.

MILLIE (*smiling*): Yes, dat was happy times. He was always doing things like dat to make people happy. (*pause*) Well dat gone now. He has gone to better places.

HELEN *enters and serves coffee to the guests.*

MARY: Anyway you still have Helen with you. She's a big girl now and can help you with things. How much years she have now?

MILLIE: Next month will give her nineteen. Yes she's really a big help to me. If it wasn't for her I don't know what I would

do. An' especially when papy was getting worse an' I had to
be with him every minute, it was she who kept this house
going. She's really a good girl.

MARY: But Millie, I don't want to ask you your business, but I
can remember hearing some people say dat besides Helen
you did have a son. Is true nuh?

MILLIE: Yes my dear, is true, But dat was so long ago I can
hardly remember dat.

MARY: So what happen to de boy now?

MILLIE: Well, my dear, three months after de chil' was born, I
wake up one morning to find dat de baby wasn't in his bed.
An den de people tol' me dat de fadder had left de village
dat morning and had take de chil' wid him. At dat time we
used to live in Coulibistrie. Since dat day I never hear a
thing about neither the fadder nor de chil'.

MARY: So you didn't know dis man's name?

MILLIE: Well, everybody used to call him Taz. Nobody knew his
real name. He had just come to Coulibistrie to do a job for
two years. He only stayed fourteen months.

MARY: Well, well, men bad.

MILLIE: If girl, I don't want to have nothing to do with dem
again, ever in my life. Although I had say dat after Cecile –
dat is what I had call my son – look what go happen wid
Helen fadder. De man leave me one year after Helen was
born. You tink I can want anything to do with men after I
take all dat from dem already? Papy was de only good man
I ever knew. An' to dis day I never let him know about
Cecile.

MARY: He never knew?

MILLIE: Never. He was living here at de time I was pregnant an'
since de man disappear wid de chil' even before I could tell
Papy, I decided to just leave it like dat. An' Papy never
found out. (*there is a knocking at the door*) Helen, see who is
dere for me please.

HELEN *opens the door. Enter* MR LINKSON, *a lawyer, with briefcase.*

LINKSON: Good night everyone, good night.
ALL: Good night.

MILLIE: Eh, Mr Linkson, I did even forget about you. Come in an' have a seat.

LINKSON: Thank you Miss Millie. Sorry I'm so late, I had intended coming for the prayers but I was kept back at the office.

MILLIE: Dat's alright, Mr Linkson. You'll take a drink?

LINKSON: Oh, no thank you. I'd rather just do what I have to do and make my way back to town. It's a long drive you know.

MILLIE: Alright, I understand. O.K. everybody; some silence please. Mr Linkson just bring ol' Papy will to read for us. So please be quiet please. (*they all motion to each other to be quiet*) Go ahead Mr Linkson.

LINKSON: Thank you, Miss Millie. Well, this is the will that old Mr Maupas wrote last October. Since he wrote it and had it all prepared he put it into my keeping to be read nine days after his death, I will now read it to you. (*he has taken the will from his briefcase and begins to read. He clears his throat*) 'This is the last will and testament of... I, John Joseph Jeremiah Maupas, I do leave all my goods and possessions to my daughter Millinette who has nursed me and cared for me during the greater part of my life. My house and two acres of land outside the village of Laudat go to her, also the animals I possess, the fowls, four pigs, six sheep, four goats and the cow.'

LIZZIE: Is two cows, Papy have.

WALIX: But is only dis year de modder cow put down. How you want Papy Maupas to know what was going to happen?

LIZ: He could have leave room for dat in de will.

WALIX: Never count your chickens before dey hatch. You don't know dat woman?

LIZ: I myself don't know what nonsense you talking about chickens, is cows dat we discussing now.

MILLIE: Eh-eh, a little cow you grudging me for. Your husband have so much things, is one cow you jealous of me for?

LIZ: Is not dat Millie, is just dat I find de will wrong. It badly make. If Papy Maupas have two cows he should say he leaving two cows for you in de will.

LINKSON: There's no need to argue over that ladies. This is just a development subsequent to the writing of the will. The two cows still go to Miss Millie.

MILLIE: You see for yourself Lizzie? De other cow is still mine. I cannot understand how other people like to put their mouth in what don't concern dem. Mr Linkson, go on with de will, you hear.

LINKSON: Yes Miss Millie. (*continues to read*) 'With reference to the money that I have in the keeping of Barclays Bank D.C.O. I also leave the sum of $800 to my daughter Millinette. (*all gasp; pause*) But there is a condition under which she must receive this money. I know my daughter to have had a long hard life with never anybody to give her real care and protection. When this will is read she will be alone in the world with only Helen, my grand-daughter, to comfort her. The two of them shall be just two lonely women left to face the world with no protection at all. To this end I have devised a way to get her a companion and a mate. Many years ago I had a friend who had done me a great service. Although this friend is now dead, I believe his son Aleck Workman to be alive and unmarried. I leave my daughter Millinette the sum of $800 on condition that she marries the son of my dear friend. In the wardrobe in my bedroom a letter can be found explaining about my friend and his son Aleck, his son's address etc. If Millinette refuses the offer, my attornies may do as they please with the money.

Signed: John Joseph Jeremiah Maupas.
Witnesses: Lawrence Caseu, and Royston Lookshaw.
Date: 30th October 19.........

There is a general silence for a while.

MILLIE: You're sure dat's what de will say, Mr Linkson?

LINKSON: Sure to the last word. (*another pause*). I'll take that drink now, Miss Millie.

HELEN: I get it for him Ma. (*she goes out*)

MARY: Millie, what you going do? (*Millie doesn't reply.*
Pause) But Millie you have to do something – what you going to do?

MILLIE: Bon Dieu, I don' know.

MARY: But look at how $800 could just slip out of a person han' like dat eh! If I had...

MILLIE (*sharply*): Who going let no money slip out of dier han'?
   Not me!

HELEN *returns with drink for* LINKSON.

MARY: But Millie, you don' hear what Papy Maupas say in de
   will? You has to marry a man for you to get the money.

MILLIE: Well, I will marry him then. What's wrong with dat?

MARY: But Millie, you just tell me you hate man so much after de
   misery dey make you see in them han'.

MILLIE: Well girl, I was just thinking about all dat myself, an'
   you know what I just come to realize? Dat men not so bad
   after all nuh! Is some women dat does make dem bad! I
   have a feeling dat dose who make me see misere had some
   woman pulling dem from me and making dem turn bad.
   Besides, girl, for $800 if Papy say to marry de devil himself I
   would marry him.

MARY (*bewildered*): Well, well! Dis earth have things, ee!

MILLIE: Ma Mary, you musn' be like dat, you know. You don't
   know you should never judge anybody without knowing de
   whole story? An' men does have a lot a story attach to dere
   dress, you know. Plenty story. So many, dat no matter how
   long you live with dem you could never find out all de story
   about dem. An' in my case neither one of dem live with me
   for longer than two years. So how you want me to just look
   at them like dat an' say dey was bad?

MARY: Excuse me. I going. My brains cannot understand dat
   kind of mathematics. (*hurriedly*) Millie, goodnight, you
   hear. I would like to stay with you a little longer but de baby
   mus' be hungry by now. See you in de morning. Goodnight
   all. (*exit*)

MILLIE: Awright, Ma Tish.

LINKSON: Miss Millie, I better be running off myself. If there's
   any business you want me to settle for you just send a note
   to my office in town.

MILLIE: O.K. Mr Linkson, thank you for coming.

LINKSON: Alright. Good night all.

ALL: Good night.

LIZ: He telling us good night, but we ourselves is time for us to go.

MILLIE: All-you going already?

LIZ: Yes, man, Millie. Is ten o'clock already and moon not shining tonight.

MILLIE: But you could all stay a little longer.

JACK: Don't worry, Miss Millie, Helen dere with you. If is anything you want in de night, jus' call out loud an' I will hear.

MILLIE: Awright Mr Jack, thank you. Well, good night all, thank you for coming an' keep praying for Papy.

ALL (*not together*): O.K. Millie, we will, good night.

Exit all except MILLIE *and* HELEN.

MILLIE: Good night.

She goes to the door to see them off. Closes the door and returns, helping HELEN *to collect the empty cups and glasses left on the chairs by the guests.*

MILLIE: Well I glad dey go. As' for dat Ma Mary, an' Miss Lizzie – always poking their nose in people's business. (*pause, then pensively*) But Papy himself was smart, you know, to thin' of a plan like dat.

HELEN: If! An' if you ask me he was too smart for me. I don't know where he got a stupid idea like dat.

MILLIE: Stupid!!! Girl you don' know what you saying! Is a first-class plan. So what you yourself thinking now, I going an' let a chance to get a husband plus $800 slip out of my han' like dat? You don' know what it is, nuh, girl, for you to be my age an' not have a husband. An' you yourself should be glad we getting somebody to help us make a better living for ourselves.

HELEN: So what we going do, Mama?

MILLIE: What we going do? Well right now go an' look in Papy wardrobe for de letter he say about in de will. (*Exit* HELEN. MILLIE *sits*) Well, well, look at how things can happen! Everybody know how I not so young an' see how in my ol' age God sending a man to put me to sit down. So long I trying to hook one of dose men around here but dey playing hard-to-get. All now dey mus' be wishing it was dey Papy had say I should have married with for dem to get in de $800 an' de land and things Papy leave me. But God punish dem though.

HELEN (*entering*): Mama, look de letter.

MILLIE: Well, read it, read it.

HELEN (*sitting and opening the letter*): 'souffriere, St Mark. Dear John, It is as my days are drawing to a close that I find a little strength to write you these few lines. I have a feeling that this is the last you will hear from me as I can hear my Maker calling me very strongly to his side. We have known each other ever since school days and although we have always lived in different parts I have always thought about you as my best friend, and since this incident of a few years ago I have felt even closer to you. Anyway, let us not talk about this incident as it is not very important but as I leave this earth I want to place my son Aleck in your hands as if he were your son. He is a big man now and can take care of himself, but to me he is still my child and my son. Although I have often tried to get him to marry and settle down, he still has not done so. Please help him if he ever needs help. You will understand what I mean. He now lives at 26 River Road, Roseau. Please write and tell him what I say. This is all I ask of you. Till we meet again, your true friend, Francis Workman.'

MILLIE: But I never hear Papy talk about no man named Workman.

HELEN: Me neither.

MILLIE: An' I wonder what accident this Francis Workman talking about.

HELEN: Not 'accident', Mama, 'incident'.

MILLIE: Well, whatever it is, I wonder what dat was.

HELEN: It mus' be dis 'great service' dat Papy say in de will dis man had do for him.

MILLIE: Maybe. I wonder what dat was anyway. (*pause, pensive for a moment*) So is de son of dis Francis Workman dat Papy want me to married to. What dey say his name is?

HELEN (*fumbling in the letter*): Aleck.

MILLIE: An' where he living?

HELEN: 26 River Road, Roseau.

MILLIE: Well, get de pen an' de pad, girl, we have to write him
tonight.

Helen gets them from the corner table up-stage right.

MILLIE: We cannot waste time with a thing like that, nuh, you
can never tell what plans some other woman have on de
poor man. (HELEN *sits at the table centre stage, places pad on it*)
You ready?

HELEN: Yes Ma.

MILLIE: Dear Mr Workman, dis is to…

HELEN: But Ma.

MILLIE: What?

HELEN: Supposing de man is much, much older dan you, or
much, much younger? (*pause*)

MILLIE: Well from what de letter say, his fadder went to school
together with Papy, so he an' Papy should have had about
de same age. An' if Papy could have had me so dat I am now
44 years…den his fadder could have had him so dat he
could be 44 years or at least something close to dat. (HELEN
looks puzzled) Anyway girl, don't worry with dat, write.
(HELEN *settles down to it again*) Dear Aleck, dis is to inform
you of your forthcoming marriage to me, one Millinette
Maupas of Laudat.

HELEN: But Mama, dat not good, you not even asking de man.
You telling him one time, oui.

MILLIE: Is not me dat tell, nuh, is you gran' fadder dat say it
have to be so.

HELEN: If you want de money!

MILLIE: Dat's right, An' I want de money, so it have to be so.

HELEN: Anyway, de way you telling him not good. You will
frighten de man, you know. You have to show more love
man.

MILLIE: So what you saying I should put den?

HELEN: Well… something like, 'Dear Mr Workman, we do not
know each other now, but the one who knows all, the great
Lord above, knows that soon, the two of us who do not
know each other now, and who have never known each
other before, shall know each other so well that the knot

that shall lie between us shall never unknit for a long time, or maybe forever, we may never know'.

MILLIE: 'Know, know, know, know! No! dat not good. It have too much 'know' in it. You will make the man say 'no' before he even know.

HELEN: Well, let me hear what you want to put now.

MILLIE: I like de part you had about de great Lord above. Things about God does always frighten people at bit....How about, 'Dear Mr Workman, de ways of de Lord are strange. Who would believe dat in a few days from now you would own two acres of land, a house, ten pigs, fourteen goats, three cows and a beautiful wife!'

HELEN: Yes. Dat good. An den all you have to put is 'For further information call at de house of Miss Millinette Maupas, Laudat Village.'

MILLIE: Um-hum. But as though I still don't like that. Anyway, we can still change it round a-little.

HELEN: But Mama, supposing Mr Workman don't want to married with you.

MILLIE: Well my chil'. Dey have a little thing; once you can put it on a man you sure bet he married with you.

HELEN: What is dat, Ma? A ring?

MILLIE: No my chil'. Dey does call it ca-coa.

Blackout.

Scene 2: *The same, a week later.*
There is knocking on the door upstage centre. A boy of about 20 years peeps through the door and then enters looking about while calling. He is Aleck Workman, better known as 'Celsy'. He is tired and hot.

CELSUS: Good morning. Good morning, Miss Millie. Miss Millie? Anybody home? (pause) So what happen now, nobody home? I hope this is the right place. But of course it must be. I read this letter three times already. (*pulls it out of his pocket*) Of course it must be here, look the part where it says 'the house of Miss Millie Maupas at Laudat, just pass the church and under the big mango tree'. So this must be

the place. (*pauses and contemplates the letter for a while*) Hum,
but that's a hell of a funny letter, oui. What a man suppose
to do in a situation like that now? He just suddenly getting a
letter telling him 'If you come Laudat an' ask for Miss
Millie Maupas you will get fowls, pigs, goats, sheep and
cows plus a pretty wife and $800!' Now what a man suppose
to do when he get a letter like that now? The offer sound
nice, but I don't even know the lady, if she pretty or not, if is
she I has to married with or what. To make it worse, look I
reach right in her house itself and not a soul around. (*pause*)
Anyway I going and call one last time an' if nobody come, I
gone. Miss Millie? Good morning Miss Millie? Anybody
home?…Anybody home? (*there is still no reply*) Well that is
that, I going. (*as he goes to the door* HELEN *enters stage right*)

HELEN: Yes? Somebody was calling?

CELSUS: Yes! I been here calling for the last half an hour. Where
you was nuh? (*he is a bit vexed*)

HELEN: We was in the garden at the back of the house weeding.
Sorry we didn't hear you.

CELSUS: Well, all-you must be deaf or something. My throat
almost come out. (*softly after a pause*) Well, me myself sorry
too. I has no right to be shouting at you like dat. After all is
not your fault if you didn't hear. (*they stare at each other. They
have fallen in love*) You know…you're a very pretty girl, you
know.

HELEN: Well –am…will you have a seat?

CELSUS (*still standing*): You're the pretties' girl I've seen for a
long time.

HELEN (*too embarrassed to stay in the room*): Am…will you have a
drink, you looking hot. I'll get one for you. (*she hurries out*)

CELSUS: Sacre tonneur! Look a preety craaf. Well, well, I would
never believe that it could happen to me but I think it's love
at first sight, oui. From the moment I see the girl I think I
fall in love with her. (*pause*) But wait…This must be the
Millie Maupas that send the letter for me. This must be the
girl I have to marry for me to get all those things she
mention, plus $800! Sacre tonneur! And see how I fall in
love with de woman even before I know it was she. Oh God,
this life have miracles in it, oui, miracles!!!

Enter HELEN *with a drink.*

CELSUS: Look Miss, I want to tell you how sorry I am for
    shouting at you like that a while ago. And, and…I. I want
    to tell you h…h…h.how much I love you already. So now
    that you see me and you know how I feel, you can tell me
    how you like me so we can see how things will turn out.

HELEN (*a bit shy*): Well, sir, I don't even know who you are, an' I
    don't even know what you talking about…what is your
    name?

CELSUS: Well…all my friends call me Celsy. You can call me
    that too. I have another name, but is Celsy everybody call
    me.

HELEN: An' where you from?

CELSUS: Well…right now I live in Roseau, by the river. But to be
    honest I was born in Coulibistrie.

HELEN: So in town you does live? With your mother and father?

CELSUS: No I does live by myself.

HELEN: By yourself?

CELSUS: Yes. For the last five years. I don't even know who my
    mother is.

HELEN: What? How come?

CELSUS: Well. It's a long story. Anyway I can explain to you
    briefly. You see, my father had me with my mother when he
    was working in Coulibistrie. But at the same time he had
    another caff in Rouseau. So when the one in town hear that
    my father had another caff in Coulibistrie and had even
    make a child with her, she get jealous and decide that she
    coming up to Coulibistrie after my father. Well, my father
    hear the news and he decide that he don't want to meet up
    with this town woman, because she was a bad woman. So
    early one morning he take me from my mother, although I
    was just a few weeks old, and we go by his father in
    Soufriere. An' for the fifteen years since is so we have been
    moving from place to place, as my father running away
    from this woman who was following him everywhere. Well,
    five years ago just after my grandfather die, he say he was
    going where it be hard for the woman to follow him and he
    left and go to Curaçao. Well, that finally stopped the

woman from following my father – I hear that she went to England last year. So since my father go away and my grandfather die, I have been living alone and up to now I don't know my mother.

HELEN: Elas, dat is a sad story.

CELSUS: Yes. Anyway that don't matter too much. Right? So now you know my whole life story tell me what you think of me.

HELEN: Well…Although I know your life story I still don't know you for very long.

CELSUS: I know, I know…but just tell me if you like me or not.

HELEN: Well to be honest…I don't mind you; but…

CELSUS: Oh glory alleluah, look how things going an' work out. Mon dieu, merci! So, Miss Millie, you don't realize that its me. It's me. Aleck Workman, who you send the letter to last week, telling me to come to your house and I will married with you this minute, just say the word.

HELEN (*astonished*): But, but…I am not…

CELSUS: I know you are not forcing me to married with you. But I want to married with you. And not for your cows and your goats and your money. I want to married with you for yourself. My father have enough money, and me myself too. I don't want your things. Is you I want. You don't understand. I think I love you.

HELEN: *You* don't understand…you see, I am not Miss Millie.

CELSUS: I don't care, I… (*pause*) wait. You are not Miss Millie? (*he is astonished*)

HELEN: No.

CELSUS: Well what you doing in this house?

HELEN: I live here.

CELSUS: And you are not Miss Millie?

HELEN: No.

CELSUS: Then who is Miss Millie?

Enter MILLIE, *angry*.

MILLIE: I am Miss Millie. An I want to know what you doing talking to my daughter like that.

CELSUS (*frightened*): Mmbb…your daughter?

MILLIE: Yes my daughter, and I don't like young boys just

coming in my house an' talking to my daughter like that.
You haven't got no manners?

HELEN *bursts into tears*.

MILLIE: Now, Helen, what happen to you, you crying like that?

CELSUS: Excuse me, ma'am. I think I can explain everything
to…

MILLIE: You shut up and keep out of this. This is business
between me an' my daughter.

HELEN: Mama! (*she is sobbing*)

MILLIE: Yes. What happen to you now.

HELEN: Mama, this is Aleck Workman.

MILLIE: Who?

HELEN: Aleck Workman, the man dat granpa say you have to
married with for you to get money.

MILLIE (*astonished*): What!!!!

CELSUS: Yes ma'am is me who is Aleck Workman who you send
the letter to.

MILLIE (*taken aback, does not know what to do or say*): Well, well, well
am…am…Will you have a seat?

CELSUS (*sitting*): Thank you.

MILLIE: You must really excuse my manners a while ago. I had
no idea that it was you, Aleck, and dose fresh boys around
here always coming behind Helen.

CELSUS (*stiffly*): That's alright.

MILLIE: Bon Dieu! I had no idea that you would come so soon;
and look at my state! (*fixes her clothes*) Anyway Aleck you get
my letter an' so on? Good. So we have to decide on a date for
the wedding one time. I think that next week Sunday would
be the best day. An I don't want too much of a big fete nuh,
just a few close friends would do. But I must have a long
white dress and my long veil because…

CELSUS: Look Miss Millie, let me tell you something. I have
absolutely no intention of marrying you. And if I have any
intention of marrying anybody in this house it is your
daughter. I hope you understand that right now.

MILLIE: What? But you crazy, nuh. You don't know what my
father put in his will nuh. Right in his will you know. He put

in that will that you have to married to me.

HELEN: If you want to get the money!

MILLIE (*attacking*): Shut up child!

CELSUS: Well, I don't care what you father say in his will I don't
even know who you father was and I don't even know how
he know about me. But one thing I know is that I am not
marrieding with you. En-en. So what you taking me for
now, some kind of cunnummu? You expecting me to
married with old woman like you? You could be my
mother.

MILLIE: I don't care what I could be. I say that I marrieding
with you and I means dat I marrieding with you. An' if you
give me any trouble let me tell you from now that I get ways
and means to force your hand.

CELSUS: Ways and means? Like what? (*a bit frightened*)

MILLIE: Never mind that, just remember that they have a lot of
power in a woman's hands.

CELSUS: O God, I feeling sick.

MILLIE: Sick you sick but jus' don't give me no trouble because
is den you going and find out what sick is.

CELSUS: Agghh. (*rushing out through kitchen as if he going to vomit,
holding mouth*)

HELEN: But Mama! How you can do that to him?

MILLIE: So how you mean. I going an' let him escape an' lose de
whole $800?

HELEN: But Mama he's so young – how you can expect to
married with him?

MILLIE: Age don't matter in dat. I getting a chance to get a man
to look after me and help me to see about de animals and de
land and I not going an' let him escape. Besides I must to
get the $800.

HELEN: Well, the way it look he don't want to married with you.

MILLIE: Don't worry with dat. As I told him, I have my ways
and means.

HELEN: So you really going an' ca-coa him?

MILLIE: Well, I'll give him a little chance still but if he continues
to play hard to get you sure bet I going and ca-coa him. An
if dat don't work – obeah next for him. Anyway, what he
worrying 'bout, nuh? I going an' die just now and he will get

all my things. He should be glad. (*pause*) Poor fella he really looking frighten, oui. Let me go and get something for him to drink.

HELEN: I had bring one for him already. Look, it dere.

MILLIE: Oh, but it must be hot, all de ice melt. Le me go an' pu' some ice in it for him. (*exit with drink*)

HELEN: Bonjay, how I have bad luck so, nuh? De first time dat I see a boy dat I really like em' he have to be de boy for my mother to married. Life have some hard times in it oui, Bonjay. I really feeling sorry for the boy…an' for myself too.

Enter CELSUS, *weakly*.

CELSUS: Well, Miss Helen, it was a pleasure meeting you. I going eh.

HELEN: You going? But you doh hear what my mother say noh boy? If you leave is obeah for you, oui.

CELSUS (*collapsing weakly in chair*): Ohhhhh. (*half crying*)

HELEN: Poor boy. I really feelin sorry for you. But de only thing I can tell you to do is to go along with what my mother say because I can tell you dat when she say she mean business *she mean business eh*.

CELSUS: Ohhhhh. (*louder*)

HELEN: Married with her man. De good Lord always work out things for the best.

CELSUS: Except dat dis time he seem to forget all about me.

HELEN: Doh say dat, nuh. I'm sure dat we can always work something out.

CELSUS: We can?

Enter MILLIE.

MILLIE: Look, your drink Aleck, I put some more ice in it for you.

CELSUS: I hope is ice alone you put in it.

MILLIE (*sucks her teeth; then, trying to be nice*): Boy you stupid, eh. Have your drink an' relax, man.

CELSUS (*on guard*): I dosen drink.

MILLIE: But how he nervous so, nuh. Relax a bit, nuh. Look, you want a cigarette? (*getting them from the table*)

CELSUS: I dosen smoke.

MILLIE: But what wrong with you nuh? You hungry? You want some food? We has a nice braff on de fire.

CELSUS (*breaking down*): I dosen eat.

MILLIE: Doh cry nuh, Aleck, I…

CELSUS: Doh call me Aleck, my name is Celsus…Celsus Aleck Workman, an' everybody does call me Celsy.

MILLIE: Awright, take it easy dou-dou. Everything going an' be fine. We going have de best wedding dat Laudat ever see…

CELSUS: In your mind.

MILLIE: …with cake an' Top Screw an' Hawan-son an' even lache-couchon.

CELSUS: Ohhhhh!

Enter a group of villagers.

MARY: Millie chil' we just hear your good news. So we rush up here one time to find out if is true.

MILLIE: Is true oui, my dear.

LIZZIE: Well you know how news can fly round this village fast. Jennie just tell us how a man just come dere asking for you so we put two an' two together an' we say dat it must be de one for you.

ANNIE: Your future husband.

MILLIE *smiles coyly.*

MARY (*looking around*): So where de man now? Dat little boy dere is his brother or his son?

MILLIE: My dear, dis is de man himself. Mr Aleck Workman, Esq.

CELSUS: Celsus.

MILLIE: Aleck Celsus Workman.

MARY: That? (*going to Celsus*) Well, my boy, let me be the first to offer my concelebrations. I had no idea dat you was de one. An' let me tell you dat you are a lucky man for you to get such a lovely wife.

MILLIE *stands next to the totally bewildered* CELSUS *as the villagers crowd round congratulating the couple.* HELEN *runs off crying as the lights fade out.*

Scene 3: *The same, two weeks later.*
CELSUS, *in an oversized suit, sits glumly on a chair centre stage, while women rush back and forth with various bits of* MILLIE's *wedding garments as they help her to dress. Enter* HELEN, *who sits.*

HELEN: Doh look so sad, nuh. Things not dat bad.
CELSUS: Well de way I seeing them they not so good either.
HELEN: Well…What to do? (*pause*) So none of your people not coming to de wedding den?
CELSUS: I tell you already, Helen, I haven't got nobody here, I was living by myself. My father right in Curaçao.
HELEN: An dat so far.
CELSUS: If! But I sure if he was here he would get me out of dis trouble, oui. He would give your mother de eight hundred dollars, if is dat she want. Or he would do something to prevent me from marrying a old woman like dat.
HELEN: So your father don't even know dat you getting married, den.
CELSUS: Well, maybe he know, oui, because as soon as I decide to marry you I write and tell him about it. I tell him dat a Millie Maupas had tie me up in a marriage business an I couldn't escape, so even if he couldn't help me maybe he could still come to de wedding.
HELEN: So maybe he will come.
CELSUS: If he get de letter. But sometime dese does take so long to reach. Maybe is next month he will get de letter. You never can tell.
HELEN: De ways of the Lord are strange.
CELSUS: I hope so, because I still looking for a way to escape. Eh!
HELEN: You not easy boy.

Enter MR JACK.

CELSUS: Eh-eh, Look de pall-bearer, oui.

HELEN: De what?

CELSUS: De pall-bearer. Mr Jack.

HELEN: Oh you mean de best-man.

CELSUS: Is a pall-bearer he is oui, because right now I feel is me funeral I going to an' is bury dey going an' bury me.

JACK: Well Aleck boy, you ready to go to church?

CELSUS: I not ready to go nowhere. An' stop calling me Aleck, my name is Celsus.

HELEN: You'll take a drink, Mr Jack?

JACK: Yes thanks, Helen.

HELEN: I'll get it for you. (*exits*)

JACK: Well, dis is an important day for you, boy. You not feeling nervous?

CELSUS: Nervous for what? People does feel nervous when dey tie up, nuh.

JACK: I can remember my wedding day as if it was yesterday. I was a young man of twenty.

CELSUS: Wait, You mean dey co-cao you too?

JACK: What?

CELSUS: You mean dey co-cao you too?

JACK: What you mean by dat?

CELSUS: Well if you married when yuh was only twenty years your wife must have co-cao you because no man in Dominica does married at dat age of his own free will.

JACK: Look, pal, I doh come here for you to insult me like dat, eh.

CELSUS: But your wife is a old soucoyant for her to co-cao you like dat, man.

JACK: What! How you can call my wife a soucoyant, nuh. (*pushes him*)

CELSUS: But dat's what she is, man. Everybody know dat. An' doh push me, man.

JACK: But you damn rude, man. (*pushes him*)

CELSUS: An' you damn stupid. Doh push me, man. (*pushes* JACK)

JACK: Oh, is fight you want?

CELSUS: Is dat so come.

They fight. Enter HELEN *with drink.*

HELEN: All you come quick, look Celsus and Mr Jack fighting.

General commotion. Enter villagers and MILLIE. *They separate the fighters.*

MILLIE: But look at two big men fighting. All-you not shame!

JACK: But he call my wife a soucoyant.

CELSUS: But is dat she is.

MILLIE: Aleck, I shame for you.

CELSUS: I glad.

MILLIE: *You* should know better dan dat.

JACK: Millie. I sorry but I not best manning dat young animal over dere. He too damn rude. Let him say nothing about Jannie again an see if I doh bust his mouth for him.

MILLIE: Whose mouth you talking about dere, nuh?

JACK: But he call my wife a soucoyant.

CELSUS: Is dat she is.

MILLIE: Dat is true. Everybody know how she sucking people blood an' how she going to Guadeloupe an' come back every first Friday.

JACK: Oh, so is so? You backing him, den?

MILLIE: Of course. I has to stand by my husband.

CELSUS: Your what?

JACK: Look at dat de boy doh even want to married wity yo, you had was to force him. You coco him your ol' soucoyant, you coco him.

MILLIE: Get out of my house you damn son of a bitch. You too damn rude an comparasion, get out.

JACK: Wif pleasure. You caco de boy, vieux soucoyant, you caco him. (*goes out*)

MARY: Well, look zafaire here today.

MILLIE: Doh worry wif dat man, dat is just part of what day does call wedding-day excitement.

MARY: I see.

MILLIE: I hope you not too upset, Aleck, dat was just small matters.

CELSUS: Me? Upset? I was too glad.

MILLIE: Dat good.

CELSUS: Of course you realize dat I cannot married you again.

MILLIE: How come?

CELSUS: But I haven't best-man. Where you ever hear about people getting married without best-man.

MILLIE: Bonjay, dat you worrying about, nuh? But look – Mr
    Walix right here. I sure he wouldn't mind. Mr Walix you
    would mind?

WALIX: Of course not, Miss Millie, with pleasure.

MILLIE: You see, matter fix. An doh even try to quarrel with dis
    one because he's not a man dat does vex and fight.

CELSUS: But I still cannot married.

MILLIE: Why?

CELSUS: Look, my jacket tear.

MILLIE: Oh Lord, how you manage?

CELSUS (*self-satisfied*): While we was fighting.

MILLIE: An' is Papy suit I had take out of de cupboard to len' de
    boy. Anyway I can fix dat. Helen, get some safety pin on my
    table for me.

Exit HELEN.

CELSUS: You mean you going pin it?

MILLIE: You expect me to sew it now? We haven't got time for
    dat.

HELEN *returns with pins.* MILLIE *starts to pin.*

CELSUS: But where you ever hear of man marrieding with pin-up
    clothes.

MILLIE: Wedding with pin-up clothes better dan no wedding.
    An' doh even worry to say more. Dis wedding taking place
    dis morning by de hook or de crook.

CELSUS: You mean by de hook *and* de crook. Because you's de old
    crook dat hook me.

MILLIE: Right, look it fix up. Now just sit down here an' stay
    cool, I going an' finish dress. I'll ready just now.

Exit MILLIE *and women.*

CELSUS (*aside*): Shocks. What de hell I going an' do now?

WALIX: What you say, pal?

CELSUS: Oh – get it. I feeling giddy. I feeling faint.
WALIX: You feeling sick?
CELSUS: I going an' faint. I going an…(*faints*)
WALIX: Millie, Helen all-you look, de boy faint!

MILLIE *and others enter.*

MILLIE: Oh Lord, look de boy die, he die, he die. Look what I go
and do to dis poor young boy.
HELEN: Is not die he die, Mama, is faint he faint.
MILLIE: Oh is faint he faint? Well all-you quick, get a bucket of
water to dash on him. Quick, it have one in de kitchen.

Exit woman to kitchen.

HELEN: You think we should really dash him, Mama?
MILLIE: But is de only way to wake him up.

Enter woman with bucket of water.

MARY: Look, de bucket, Millie.
MILLIE: Gimme O.K. Everybody step back. (*swings bucket*)
one…two…th…
CELSUS (*getting up*): O.K. Doh worry, doh worry. I falling sick
enough before I go catch pneumonia with all-you ol' col'
water.
MILLIE: Boy is joke, you was joking.
CELSUS: No. Is dead I was dead.
MILLIE: Boy, you mustn't do things like dat you know you nearly
give me heart failure dere.
CELSUS: I better do it again den. (*attempts*)
MILLIE: Doh try dose kind of jokes again, eh. Look, it look like
you really trying to get away now, you might even try to run
through de door just now. But I 'ready tell you what will
happen to you if you try dat. As a matter of fact I staying
right here an' make sure you doh try no false move. Is only
my veil to put on now an we ready to go. All-you quick, get
it for me.

MILLIE *does her final dressing on one side of the stage.*

CELSUS: No, but I was really feeling sick, oui.

MILLIE (*sarcastically*): Oh yes, sweetheart.

CELSUS: For true – an up to now I not too steady. Helen, you haven't got a drink dere.

HELEN: It had one dere I had bring for Mr Jack.

CELSUS: Doh even call mister name for me.

HELEN (*giving drink*): Look it.

CELSUS: Thank you. Well, here's to the memory of my boyhood days of happiness, joy peace an' contentment. It was a good life but de Lord see it fit to take me away from it. As I say goodbye to happiness, let it not be said that I did not do my good turn for a old miserable woman like Miss Millie, but let it be hoped dat one day I might rise again from the valley of dispair an' come out with eight hundred dollars.

As he drinks he spills the drink on his jacket.

CELSUS: Oh Lord, look at how my shirt get wet down.

MILLIE: What?

CELSUS: Well it doh seem I can get married again.

MILLIE (*coming over*): Why?

CELSUS: But look at my jacket. It wet down. How I can get married in a wet suit, nuh.

MILLIE: You doh know, well you'll soon find out because you going an' do it just now. (*to woman*) Take dat cloth on de table for me. (*to* CELSUS) You have too many tricks in your skin. You not escaping. Look, I wiping the suit for you. You see, it good. An before anything else happen let us go to de church right now. I ready.

CELSUS: You coming *now*?

MILLIE: Yes. I not leaving you alone from now on – you trickster. You will try something else.

CELSUS: But how you can come now nuh. De man suppose to go in de church first and wait on de woman to come. Dat is tradition.

MARY: Dis going an' be de best wedding Laudat ever see.

CELSUS (*aside*): So you mean I really going an' get hang today, eh. Eh ben oui, I only wish my father was here. Well God, is you alone dat know what you doing. (*To* HELEN, *who is close by*) Helen…I don't know what to say. I only wish…

WALIX: Wait Millie, before all-you go let me take out a few pictures, man. Dis is a day must not be unforgettable.

MILLIE: Well…awright. We still have some time. Where to stand up?

WALIX: Over here. A little more so.

All the villagers crowd round MILLIE *and* CELSUS *trying to get into the picture. They take five or six in to get in different poses. During this time there is knocking at the door, but the people are too taken up to hear it. Finally a small boy hears, goes to the door and speaks to someone who we can't see, then returns to the group.*

MILLIE: O.K. Walix, dat enough.

WALIX: One more, one more…good.

MILLIE: Right so much for dat. Everything ready, man?

MARY: Yes Millie.

MILLIE: Let us go.

SMALL BOY: Miss Millie, while all-you take-outing de picture an dem somebody was knocking.

MILLIE: Who it was!

SMALL BOY: I donno, a man. He say he was looking for a boy dey calling Celsy.

MILLIE: An what you tell him?

SMALL BOY: I tell him dat dey haven't got nobody dey calling Celsy here.

CELSUS: But how…

MILLIE: Quiet. (*to boy*) Where de man go?

SMALL BOY: He say he going an ax order piple because he come all de way from Curaçao to make sure his son don't commit de greatest crime in de world.

CELSUS: (*breaking loose and running out through door centre*): Daddy!

MILLIE: Daddy? All-you quick an' follow him. It might be another trick he trying to escape. (*exit some villagers*) (*to boy*) But boy how you stupid so. You donno Celsy is de man I going an marry now?

SMALL BOY: I never hear nobody call him like dat. Is Aleck I hear everybody calling him.

MILLIE: Next time make sure somebody else go an' open de
door, eh!

Enter CELSUS, *hugging his father,* ALECK.

CELSUS: Daddy, I was just praying for you to come, man. At
least I would have one relative at dis wedding.
ALECK: Well Celsy boy, I had to come because dis wedding have
to stop. I...
MILLIE (*thunderstruck when she sees* ALECK): Taz!
ALECK: Millie!

They rush to each other.

MILLIE: Oh, Taz. I know you would come back one day, I knew.
I knew. Twenty years we don't see, but I knew.
ALECK: Millie is you one I always loved, you know dat.
CELSUS: But...but...but what happening dere, nuh.
ALECK: What happening? Boy, you don't know who dis lady is?
Dis is your own mother.
CELSUS: M...M...my what?
ALECK: Your mother.
CELSUS: My mother? (*shocked*)
MILLIE: Y...you mean dat dis same boy I was going
an' married with dere is my son?
ALECK: Yes Millie, your son.
MILLIE: My own son?
ALECK: De same little boy I had stole from you in Coulibistrie.
MILLIE: But Taz, why you had do dat for, nuh?
ALECK: Well, is a long story, man. Dey had a woman running
after me an' I didn't want her to meet me so I had to run.
MILLIE: But why you had to take de baby nuh, Taz?
ALECK: Man, I know he would be a burden for you to bring up so
I decide to take him with me.
MILLIE: Mary, you see what I was telling you about woman
making man do bad thing.
CELSUS: An' den is den we had go to Soufriere?
ALECK: Yes, we go to Soufriere by my father, an' I tell him de
whole story. I tell him how I love you. An' since he an' you

use to be such good friends he write an' tell your father
everything. An de two of dem even say dat dey going an'
work out something for de two of we to married.

MILLIE: Oh, so dat is why Papy set up de will like dat. But he had
tell me to write to Aleck Workman – your…I mean…our
son.

ALECK: No man, is me dat is Aleck Workman. I call my son
Celsus Aleck after me. But I was de first.

MILLIE: So is you Papy had mean.

CELSUS: But I get de letter by mistake since me an' my father
have de same name, an' I was living where he used to live.

MILLIE: But I never knew it was Aleck dat was your name.
Everybody call you Taz.

ALECK: Because I was strong like Tarzan.

MARY: Well, well, well, eh bien mi zafaire.

MILLIE: Anyway, my son, I more dan glad I didn't married with
you. Come, let me hug you.

CELSUS: An' Mama, I cannot find words to say how I happy!
(*they hug*)

ALECK: Well…well…Millie, since everything ready for de
wedding already, you…you…think you will marry *me*
instead?

MILLIE: Bonjay Taz – the pleasure is yours.

She hugs him – all cheer, except CELSUS *who looks sad.*

ALECK: But Celsy boy, how you looking so sad? You not happy
dat all dis work so.

CELSUS: Yes Daddy, I glad how I find my mother an' how you
come back an' how you stop disaster. But I sad to see how
Helen is my own sister…I did love her so much.

MILLIE: Well, since all cat out of de bag I can bring dis one out
too. I have news for all-you. Helen is not my daughter. (*all
shocked, various exclamations*) She is my sister Moreen chil'.
When we was in Coulibistrie, just after Taz had steal
Celsus from me, Moreen got pregnant for a old schoolteach-
er an' she was so shame she didn't want my father to
know. So as soon as she make de baby she only leave de
baby for me an' she go to England. An' ma now was too

shame to let Papy know dat Taz had steal Celsus from me so
I only take Helen an' I came here to Laudat to meet Papy
an' I just tell him dat Helen was de baby I had made.

CELSUS: So you mean, Helen is not your child.

MILLIE: Correct.

CELSUS: So we can married.

MILLIE: De haven't got no law against dat.

CELSUS: Oh glory, allelooo-ya. Helen girl, look how things work
out for us. (*they embrace*)

HELEN: Celsy, I so happy I could cry.

ALECK: Well dis morning is a double wedding. Me an' Millie,
Celsy an' Helen.

MILLIE: De biggest an best Laudat ever see..

ALECK: Well, what we waiting for?

MILLIE: Let us go.

They start to leave but are stopped by CELSUS.

CELSUS: But wait. I was just thinking dere. If Miss Millie is my
mother an' Helen is Mama sister child, den Helen is my
first cousin. You think we can still married, nuh?

ALECK: Wait boy, you don't know what de good book say?

ALL: Cousin and cousin does make dozen.

*They all start to sing 'Good Morning Miss Millie' as the jubilant party
leave for the church. The bells begin to ring.*

CURTAIN

Textual notes

The language of the play

The play is set in rural Dominica and the language is that of the folk of that island. In Dominica most rural persons are (at least) bilingual in the sense that they speak a French-based creole as well as an English-based creole.

This English-based creole, when it is spoken by the folk, is strongly influenced by the lexis (vocabulary) and, to a lesser extent, the syntax (grammar) of the French-based creole. This is reflected in the play. A number of examples of this are listed below.

The items in the play that provide most problems and which need explanation or translation fall into three categories:

(a) French-creole phrases and exclamations: for example, 'oui', 'Helas', 'Bon Dieu';

(b) (Dominican) English-creole phrases and words: for example, 'all you' 'craft', 'connumunnu' (which is common to most other territories);

(c) Unfamiliar creole constructions and pronunciations: for example, 'sheeps and dem', 'going an', 'women does make men bad', 'wif' (for with), 'braff' (for broth).

Detailed notes

Page:

89   all-you: English-creole plural of you – similar to Jamaican 'unu'.

89   sheep an' dem: English-creole plural of sheep.

89   How much years she have?: How old is she? (the construction derives from the French).

107   wif: with (creole pronunciation).

90   If, girl: 'If' here connotes agreement – 'you can say that again'.

       Cecile: pronounced 'Sess-ile'. The pronunciation of the name is influenced by the French.

       Papy: pronounced 'Pappy'.

       Helas!: Interjection, 'Alas'.

Sacre tonneur: creole exclamation.
98   craaf: (good looking young) woman.
100   Elas: same as 'Helas'.
      Mon Dieu, merci: Thanks be to God.
102   cunnummu: a foolish person (especially in affairs of the
      heart).
103   Bonjay: Same as 'Bon Dieu'.
104   braff: broth.
      dou-dou: (derived from 'doux' meaning sweet), a term of
      endearment.
      Top screw: A creole delicacy.
      Hawan-son: smoked herring.
      Lache-couchon: Pig's tail.
106   soucoyant: a female vampire (belonging to eastern Carib-
      bean folklore).
107   vieux: old.
      zafaire: confusion, trouble, 'scandal'.
110   Eh bien oui: Well, yes.
111   dey calling: called.
112   you one: you alone.
113   eh bien mi zafaire: what a state of affairs.

Questions for the class or cast

1. (*pages* 88–91) What is the mood among the mourners at the
   beginning of the play? Are these all genuine mourners?
   What are their relationships with each other and with
   Millie?

2. (*page* 89) 'Boy, I had never eat so much pork before.' Does
   this tell us something about Mary, or is it a cheap joke?

3. (*page* 94) What does the dialogue on pages 94–7 suggest
   about the relationship between Millie and Helen?

4. (*page* 90) Judging from her report here, what have Millie's
   experiences with men been like? Does it seem, at this point,
   as if these experiences have seriously affected her outlook on
   life?

5. (*page* 90) What reason does Millie suggest here for not
   having told her father about Cecile? What are the other
   reasons for this decision suggested later in the text?

6. (*page* 91) Do you think that Millie really forgot that the lawyer was to come to read the will? If so, what does this tell us about her? If not, why does she say so?

7. (*pages* 90–3) From the little that we see of Mr Linkson, what conclusions can we come to about his personality?

8. (*page* 91) Why was the will to be read nine days after Papy's death? How does this ensure that his friends would all be present at the reading?

9. (*page* 91) What motivation could Lizzie have for seeing a problem in the will? Is she simply jealous or could it be a more complex personality feature. If it is the latter, how could an actress playing the role use this to help create an interesting character?

10. (*page* 93) Is Millie really as much of a money-grabbing hypocrite as she seems here? Does she plan to use a husband to get the money or to use the money to get a husband?

11. (*page* 93) What should Mary's body language say here? Would she reveal anything to Millie with her face, gestures or body attitude?

12. (*page* 94) 'You could all stay a little longer.' At this point, would Millie show or conceal her desire for them to leave? Whatever the choice, how could an actress demonstrate it?

13. (*page* 96) 'you can never tell what plans some other woman have on de poor man'. What is the irony here?

14. (*page* 96) Why does the writer pause to underline the idea that Aleck Workman should be around Millie's age? How does it tie in with the rest of the plot?

15. (*pages* 96–7) What do we learn about the personalities of the two protagonists from their discussion of the letter?

16. (*pages* 97–8) What first impression of Celsus should the audience receive? Is he hot and tired, or cool and handsome or what? How can answers to this question help the actor in his creation of the character?

17. (*page* 98) 'They have fallen in love.' Is Helen shy at this point? Is Celsus? How does Helen respond to him: shy? What about Celsus? Is he shy or is he self-confident but a bit taken aback by her attractiveness?

18. (*page* 98) Is Helen's exit an escape? If so is it from Celsus or

from her own confused emotions?

19. (*pages* 101–4) How would Celsus react (physically) while Millie is outlining her plans: does he sneer, does he not take her seriously or is he resolute?

20. (*page* 102) Helen's remark, 'If you want to get the money!' is an attack on her mother. (a) Is it the first time we see this aspect of her? (b) In what way could an actress prepare the audience for this moment so that it does not come too suddenly? (c) What would be the most effective way for her to deliver this line?

21. Is Millie sinister, desperate, scheming, simply determined or what? Is what goes on inside her commendable, understandable, or despicable?

22. (*pages* 102–3) What is Helen's 'internal action' during the 'ca-coa him' sequence (that is, what emotions does she feel): In what ways could her body language reveal (or try to conceal) this internal action?

23. (*page* 103) Helen: 'Poor boy. I really feelin sorry for you.' Does this sum up her feelings or is there much more?

24. (*page* 103) What do we learn about Helen in this exchange with Celsus?

25. (*page* 104) During her statement at the end of the scene what should Mary's body language tell us?

26. (*page* 105) What is the symbolism in Celsus's oversized suit?

27. (*page* 105) 'You not easy boy.' Is this said with pride (as praise)? As a consolation or cynically?

28. (*page* 107) To whom is the statement '*You* should know better dan dat' addressed?

29. (*page* 108) Is Celsus' humour when he says 'de old crook dat hook me' wry, dismayed or angry?

30. (*page* 110)   How could an actress point the line 'Dis going an be de best wedding Laudat ever see'?

31. (*page* 111) How could a director use the (unanswered) knocking on the door to: (a) show the excitement of the crowd; (b) prepare the audience for the denouement?

32. (*page* 113) 'An Mama I cannot find words to say how I happy!' When Celsus calls her 'Mama' how does this reverberate? What do we remember? How does it 'fit' him and her?

Production notes

Set design

(*a*) In a play of this nature it is easy for the design to be a cliché. The author suggests to us the stereotype of a country home, but leaves enough clues for us to realize that there are features that give the house some personality of its own.

(*b*) An interesting classroom (rehearsal) exercise that can be undertaken is for the class to design the house in realistic detail, then redesign it for the stage – bearing the advantages and limitations of the theatre in mind. (Making a model can be a helpful group exercise – and it is often fun.)

(*c*) If one is staging the play for a festival – where one has to mount (put up) and strike (take down) the set in a short space of time – a number of questions must be addressed, for example, 'Will we use walls?' If so are we going to imply that the walls are concrete or wooden (as 'partition' seems to imply)? If we are not going to use walls how will we create the 'feel' of the house – in terms of space as well as its ambience?

(*d*) 'What details of decorations are we going to use?' is also a significant question. Decisions on the furnishing of the house can be approached by assuming that Millie's personality would rub off on her house. So to decide on the fittings, decorations and so on we need to examine/create Millie's character. (This is also useful as a classroom exercise because one is here using a practical, 'life' situation in one's contemplation of the details of character. This helps the student to see the character as a person.) The pictures on the walls or standing on the furniture should be real pictures of Millie, Helen (the actresses in costume), and Papy. A calendar or a poster could indicate the year and country in which the play is set. Minor alterations to actual calendars could achieve this.

(*e*) 'Does the house have electricity?' The answer to this question has implications for deciding how deeply rural this village community actually is. If the answer is no, then a lamp should be placed somewhere on the set and be already lit at the opening of the play. The stage manager needs to assign someone to see that it is lit in all night scenes and put out during day scenes (or the director can give an actor the job of blowing out the lamp as part of his stage business).

(*f*) 'How well off was Papy?' In a poor community Papy may have been above average, as he leaves a sum of money that seems quite large to the villagers. The answer to this question, though, has implications for the type of table and chairs that are on the set, the cups that Helen brings in, and so on.

In creating the set the design should be one which gives people room to move – nothing that is purely decorative should be used if it results in a problem in terms of space, and everything that is used should be set in such a way that actors can move around comfortably. This must be so even if one is attempting to give the feel of a small cluttered space.

Chairs must be set in such a way that if people sit in them they do not mask themselves, block spaces where other people move, or find themselves masked when other persons stand in natural acting areas. (You are 'masked' when the audience cannot see you properly.) At the same time one should avoid setting chairs and tables in an obviously unnatural manner as this destroys the credibility of the set. One advantage of making a cardboard model is that one can experiment with and decide on things like this long beforehand. Doors, too, should open in a direction which avoids too much loss of playing area every time they are opened. You may choose to leave an opening for the entrance to the kitchen rather than to use a door. A hanging curtain could mask the backstage area and add some extra colour to the room as well.

Costumes

The costumes of these country people can reveal their rustic nature, but a designer should be careful to avoid the temptation to make the country folk look ludicrous for no other reason than to get a laugh.

The villagers change during the action of the play from mourners in sombre colours (which may stand out in the zestful, cheerful set), to revellers who would in their brighter colours reflect and help the feel/rhythm of a play which should 'bounce' along.

Costumers often see it as a problem to arrange for an item

of clothing to be torn at every performance of a play. In this play Celsus's jacket has to be torn during his scuffle (page 106). One way of solving this is to use a jacket which is pre-torn and repaired with velcro in such a way that the tear is not visible. When the jacket is tugged the audience hears a rasping sound and sees the rip. With careful practice this can be done quite deftly.

Some points to consider

Cues for characterization

In a play like this the character types, the situations and the conflicts are easily recognizable. It is a real temptation for actors to play stereotypes and to 'ham' their way through the performance.

This is exacerbated by the fact that performances of this nature – especially if played with gusto – are often great fun for both the players and audience, so one is tempted to leave it at this. Doing so is usually a pity, as it deprives the young player of the opportunity to create a 'real' character.

Although one may wish not to take the plot too seriously and to send up the characters, this does not mean that serious work ought not to be done by the actors. A reasonable approach is to create a rounded and fairly believable character, choose those aspects of the character that one wishes to send up and then do so with a vengeance.

In the section 'Questions for the class or cast', a number of questions are asked which are meant to lead the actor/student to a broader and deeper understanding of each character.

The villagers are not, in this play, simply one character – a chorus – but are a collection of individuals who respond in different ways to the events of Millie's life. It is the total, collective reactions of these separate individuals that make up what seems to be a collective – but more complex and interesting – response. Actors in the smaller parts need to work out their individual personalities and their relationships with all the other persons in the play and dovetail this into the general 'feel' of the village.

Pacing

This play is a romp. It must 'move' always – and move with
bounce and verve. It is the type of play at which youngsters
excel because they can often effortlessly throw into it a kind of
exuberance that professional adults have to work very hard to
achieve.

The storyline cannot bear any ponderous or even 'deliberate'
forward movement. Played lightly and with charm it works
well. All else that is needed is for the lines, especially the
important ones which reveal the secrets of plot, to be enunciated
clearly and projected to the back of the house.

Important moments

There are moments when the lines being said are of extreme
importance and whatever is taking place onstage should be
made to highlight what is said. The contents of the various
letters should be clearly read, and explanations which lead to
plot twists and to the denouement need also to be clearly spoken
as they 'tell' the story.

The closing moment in Scene 1 should be carefully worked
out for its full dramatic/comic effect. The timing of the moment
and the body positions of the actors are a key to its success.

They have fallen in love (page 98). The actors/director should
work on the staging and timing for this moment to convey the
fact (which is only given in the stage directions – not expressed
in words) clearly to the audience.

Pages 100–1 includes another moment where the 'theatre' is
key. The actresses and director should consider the three
elements: the realization by Celsus that Helen is not Millie;
Millie's entry and announcement that she is Helen's mother;
and Celsus's statement that he is Aleck Workman. They should
be experimented with and staged most carefully – properly done
it could be hilarious.

The moment of recognition between Millie and Taz (page
112) also merits careful staging. The two characters must be kept
in focus – no masking, no cluttering of the stage. Timing must
be 'dead on'. The villagers should react in character – these

reactions may be very amusing to the audience – but this must be controlled, and not played out so much as to distract the audience's attention from the revelations that follow.

Crowd moments: (1) When Helen returns with the biscuits and coffee (page 89), everyone on stage can have some 'business' to do – Helen serving or people helping themselves, and so on. This helps to get the play off at a nice pace, by not allowing the stage picture to get static and dull – but one must avoid a feel of confusion or 'busyness'.

(2) The taking of the pictures (page 111). Sending this up should be a director's/actor's romp – have fun!

(3) There are moments when the script calls for improvised speech on the part of the villagers (for example, pages 105 and 111). It may be better to improvise and then 'set' these during rehearsal and not 'ad lib' at the time of performance. 'Ad libbing' may result in more spontaneity but if it is overdone by exuberant performers this can throw the play out of rhythm.

Opening and closing: the first and last moments in a play are important. They set the tone in the first instance, and leave the final impression on the mind of the audience in the second.

A director may choose to begin with the persons on stage singing the last stanza of a hymn, or doing something of that nature, which would further help to set the atmosphere. Interesting lighting and grouping would also help to create a strong start.

For the end of the play it may be advisable to compose new and suitable lyrics for a bright folk tune – this would lend authenticity and, if a suitable tune is chosen, it would help to create the gay, festive spirit that the ending calls for. The actors can react in character to the 'happening' at the end (simply as a 'single-minded' group), as this would maintain the individuality of the characters and give the actors the added satisfaction of creating as fully rounded a character as possible.

Changing the locale

If a director chooses to change the locale in which the play takes place certain amendments may have to be made:

(1) the language may have to be adjusted to the new place;

(2) the place names will have to be changed;

(3) other details, like the name 'Barclays Bank', may not be appropriate (does this bank operate in the territory in which the village has been placed?);

(4) the sum of eight hundred dollars ($800.00) may have to be reconsidered as it may seem too small to cause consternation.

Many teachers would agree, though, that there is not really very much reason for changing the locale here. 'Jamaicanization', 'Barbadianization' or 'Trinidadization' of a script may have advantages sometimes, but in a play of this nature little is gained and one suspects that something is lost. They may prefer to allow the youngsters to have fun with the creole!

4 *The Drum-Maker*

by Kendel Hippolyte

The Drum-Maker is rapidly becoming regular fare at drama
festivals in Jamaica. It is eminently 'playable' the size of the cast
is flexible (12–25 players), the subject matter is of interest to
most young people and it plays for about 50 minutes – which fits
into the normal time-frame allotment for a festival production.

It can be argued, though, that this play is even more valuable
as a classroom text than it is as a theatre-piece. The issues that
arise as a concomitant of Jack's quest are those that concern
most sensitive – and sensible – people in the Caribbean and the
Third World.

The play is powerful and in some ways disturbing. One of its
main values is that it can serve as a reassurance to the young
that the idealism of youth is not necessarily a silly phase to be
outgrown as soon as possible. In the society which the play
describes, Jack is seen as mad by other people because he has a
vision (or view of life) in which money and material possessions
are not important considerations in the life of a person or of a
society. Mr Hippolyte brings us to the point where we are forced
to consider whether Jack's voice is, in fact, the voice of sanity
and of reason.

The central character – Jack, the drum-maker – is one who
bears a resemblance to a figure who appears in the work of
many Caribbean writers. He is the outsider, the man of nature,
uneducated, not yet corrupted by the society in which he lives,
and who is still tied by an umbilical cord to the source of true
understanding, to a 'real' vision. It could prove interesting to
compare Jack with other characters who fall into the general
type, like Derek Walcott's Makak (in *Dream on Monkey
Mountain*) and Chantal (in *Malcouchon*), Sam Hilary's Rasta
Man (in *Chippy*), Roderick Walcott's Benjy (in *The Harrowing of
Benjy*) or like Mais's John Power (in the novel *Brother Man*) and
Jake (in *Black Lightning*).

Jack, like these other characters, is not a mystical, 'unreal'

125

character. He has been given enough flesh and blood to be played fairly well by most sensitive young actors.

The plot traces the changes in his life and the development of a relationship between himself and the narrator. At the beginning, the narrator is a boy who wishes to learn to play the drum (and this, one soon realizes, has symbolic significance). The boy's mother understands his wishes but sees the need for him to go to school and learn the things necessary for a life of physical well-being instead of his learning to play the drum.

The people of that part of the town are afraid because the slum-landlord plans to sell the land for the building of highly capital-intensive factories and a shopping centre. The land-owner and investor give the residents very little time to get off the land and Jack, the drum-maker, starts 'stirring up trouble' among the people by questioning their right to handle human beings like this.

The story unfolds as the people are forced to drift away and Jack keeps trying to discover the answer to the question that has plagued him from the beginning – 'who is in charge?' – of their lives, their destinies, their selves. His efforts to find the answer take Jack to the politician, the pastor, the businessman, who all talk the same language – one which Jack cannot understand or accept.

It is at this point that he starts understanding what the 'serpent' that seems to dominate their lives is made up of. It is also at this point, ironically, that the society becomes convinced that he is mad.

The Drum-Maker

A play in three movements

Characters

JACK, the Drum-maker
NARRATOR (as man and boy)
Boy's MOTHER
MERCHANT
LANDOWNER
TONY
FRANK
PASTOR
HUGHES, a businessman
4 passers-by
2 women

Set

A street scene, with bus stop to one side.

Movement 1

Darkness, steady and silent, for as long as the audience can take it. Then
JACK's *voice comes out of the darkness.*

JACK: No, I not singing. I NOT SINGING! Beg you two
shilling. Beg you fifty cent. (*puzzled*) What you doing there?
(*laughter, harsh and dry*) SSssss. You not working for the
snake? What the snake say? SSsss. Woy! Kill it, kill it! No,
no, no, no, no, doan let it touch me! You smell the money in
their hand? You smell it? Beg you fifty cent. Why you put
his face on the fifty cent? SSsss. (*painful laughter*) SSsss.

127

In the middle of this, the lights come up slowly. People have already begun coming on, heading for the bus-stop. Sounds of voices, hurrying; only a few bother to react to Jack noticeably.

PASSER-BY 1: Wha' wrong wid him?

PASSER-BY 2: So him go on all the while, me sis. Certain time the sickness hold him and won' let him go.

PASSER-BY 1: Him make too much dam' noise. Although he cyah really do better all the same.

PASSER-BY 3: Him a get worse though. He use to talk a bit o' sense one time. You coulda listen to him, still. But right now, cha! He mussy gettin' ole, all the same.

Voices continue, diminishing as they cross the stage. The last passer-by comes on while they are leaving, noticeable by his unhurried walk. Quite naturally, he begins to address the audience. He is the NARRATOR.

NARRATOR: Him no old to that. But he see too much, y'know. When a man see too much, he jus see too much – brains get a beating. In the city, dem t'ings happen all the while. The madness everywhere: on the street and sidewalks, in the bus, inside your own shirt and pants…and yet when you check it, who is a madman? (*looks back towards* JACK, *musing*)…Probably it doan even make sense to tell you? Probably you won' even understand. And then again, I might miss the last bus.

He moves hesitantly offstage. JACK*'s voice is audible now, as before.* NARRATOR *comes back on stage, a different mood, a driven decision.*

NARRATOR: I want to tell you. I want to tell you in such a way that you cyah get to sleep a night-time. And if you sleep, I want to trouble your dream. I want you walking around in the daylight with your eyes red and full of hot sand, so that you cyah close dem. You dream too much. You sleep too dam' much. Me? I cyah sleep, Jack. Sake o' Jack I cyah sleep. Him never mad though. Just see too much. I myself never see what him was saying till I start understand this network – and who make the net. But is a long time him trying to

make me see. From I was a little boy and he have his house
in the little village outside Moffat estate.

JACK *has begun to stir, as if surfacing from a sleep. His action parallels
the narration.*

Every morning, him get up before the sun, put his big bag
over his shoulder and gone.

JACK *is moving offstage by this time.*

Where him gone? (*laughs drily*) Even from that time, they
have story about him. He t'ief pickney put in there; him t'ief
money put in there; him have gold. He laugh when I ask
him and tell me everybody know him is a drum-maker and
he must make drum from what he can get, not what he
woulda like get. (*shrugs*) Always answer things in him own
way. And in those days he was always beating the drum....

*A low rolling that builds to a crescendo, then the drumming explodes, dying
to a raging stammer. The* NARRATOR *has slipped off-stage.* JACK *comes
on, a meditative rhythm on the drum hanging from his shoulder. A young
boy* (NARRATOR) *approaches from the other side. Smiling,* JACK *fades
out the rhythm.*

BOY: How you make it sound so strong? Everybody hear you.
JACK: I want everybody hear me. Drums mus' sound strong
    make everyone hear. And see.
BOY: I wish I could play loud like that.
JACK (*laughing*): Is alright. When you have things to say, you will
    want to play louder than that. You will want the whole
    world hear you.
BOY (*laughing*): How the whole world can hear me? Not even in
    the city out there so they can hear you. And look how loud
    you playing. See? Is not true.
JACK (*serious*): They doan want to hear me. Is not because I not
    playing loud enough. They doan want to hear. (*he hits the
    drum, startlingly*) And it doan matter how loud I hit the
    drum. They listening to other things. They 'fraid to hear it.

'Fraid what will happen when they hear it.

BOY: You always saying some funny things. When you going teach me to play?

JACK (*smiling*): When you want the whole world hear you. And what you have to say.

BOY: You too smart. You just doan want teach me....

JACK (*serious again*): No, not that. I didn't say when it hear you. I say when you want it hear you. No matter what, is only a few does listen. But when you play, you must want everybody hear, otherwise you will get discourage and want to stop play. I doan want you wake up the drum and then ask it to go back go sleep – it won't go back.

The BOY *is about to answer when a voice, his* MOTHER*'s calls to him from off-stage.*

MOTHER: Junior! Junior!

BOY: I over here!

MOTHER: Junior!

BOY: Over here!

MOTHER: Where?

BOY: Come this way. Mama! Listen to the drum and just follow the sound.

He happily taps out a rhythm on the drum. His MOTHER *comes in. An intense, soft-spoken woman, wise, grimly resigned to misery.*

MOTHER: You always want to play drum. Why you won't stay one place for two minute, Junior? As you come from school so, you gone again. And I know you must have homework to do.

BOY: You hear what I was playing? I play it good?

MOTHER: You play it boss, first-class. Now, go eat your food, y'hear. I put it on the table for you.

The BOY *gives the drum a resounding thump before he hurries off.*

BOY: Soon come. (*exits*)

MOTHER: You musn't encourage him, Jack, you know that

already.

JACK: I doan have to encourage him. The drum call him.

MOTHER: But you must tell him doan listen. Drum cyah feed him, cyah put roof over him head, nor shoes on him foot. Drum is crosses! Tell him that when he come round trying to play it.

JACK *stares at her silently.*

MOTHER: Tell him that! Is only the little education can help him now. To shit, I doan want him turn floor-mat and I doan want him turn thief. He must be able to help himself and live as decent somebody. Drum! What drum can do for him? Jack, we love the drumming you does do in the little village here. It make we spirit lift up, it make we remember who we is, but – look how you live. How the whole o' we live. From day to day like bird and dog. Nobody no care 'bout we. We have to make our own way, how we can –

JACK: You talking like I doan know all that! Is me you talking to, you know.

MOTHER: Yes, but what you doing?

JACK: You know how much I want do? How much time I think of how much thing? You know how much dream and intention inside this drum, bursting to come out?

MOTHER: It won't come out! It cyah come out! Dem dream going stay there and dry up and get slack like old goatskin. Dem won' die. Dem will just wrinkle and turn ugly till you cyah bear to see dem....Jack, we is nothing. Anywhere we go, we is nothing. We born down here so – lower-class. And dem mean we to dead down here so.

JACK: Shut your- Woman, shut-your-ass. I? Is I you calling nothing? You let dem fool you, make you say such a thing?

MOTHER: Is true. Ain't is true?...You doan have no power, Jack. You can send Junior go school?

JACK: What use he go school?

MOTHER: What use he doan go? What you want him do? What you can do for him?

JACK (*considering*): At school, dem will make him turn against you. Forget how his own heart start beating....

MOTHER: I make up my mind for that. My mind tighten up already. Any blow life give me, I can take it. My mind will play any rhythm it like....Cause I not in charge of what happening to my life, you understand, Mr Jack? And you not dam' well in charge of your own, neither.

JACK (*as much to himself as to her*): Is who? Is who? My heart and memory making one beat, my foot walking to a different one. Is who in charge? Who ruling me? Who have the power in this stinking place? Who? Is that I want find out!

A silence. They look at each other.

MOTHER: You hear Mr Moffat planning to sell the land?

JACK *is silent.*

MOTHER: I have to see that Junior do his homework. (*she leaves*)

After she leaves, JACK*'s meditation finds expression in his drum. A slow reflective rhythm, as when he came on, builds to a roll and an angry raging explosion as he walks off.* NARRATOR *comes back on stage.*

NARRATOR: I think was from that time the business about power start troubling him. He still playing his drum and making dem, but even me at the time could see he different. Although Moffat never sell the land that year – was just another rumour. Still, it worry Jack deep. He treat me funny like I know something or other and wouldn't tell him, y'know? When I get a scholarship to go high school, Jack tell me to find out, first thing, where the power coming from. He say I must ask the teacher, ask everybody, ask principal. He say the principal must know. Of course, me never ask no-one a dam' thing. Me too glad to get in de school in de first place, never mind to go and ask dem kinda question – make people say me facety and start notice me. No, me never say a word about 'power'. Never understand a word. I only begin to understand the year I had to leave school and start working. Two years ago, when Moffat finally sell the land and we had to move.

Towards the end of his speech, voices are heard offstage, becoming more and more audible. As the MERCHANT *and* LANDOWNER, MOFFAT, *come on stage, he glances at them and fades away. The* MERCHANT *is brisk, purposeful, the* LANDOWNER *somewhat hesitant, not as enthusiastic.*

MERCHANT: Let's not waste too much time over this. All the papers have been drawn up already? You've notified the people?

LANDOWNER: Well…not all of them are ready to move. It really was rather short notice and some of them still don't believe…But dammit after all! It's my land, I bought it. These people are stubborn. I wonder if you couldn't just give them a couple months more –

MERCHANT: Out of the question! It's taken enough time already. My contractor is ready to start this week if necessary. And he's hinted to me already that I'm keeping him from other jobs. Dammit man. You won't get another offer like mine. Not in a hurry.

LANDOWNER: I know, I know.

MERCHANT: So what you waiting for?

LANDOWNER: Well…It's just that…

MERCHANT: Don't tell me you're worrying about what will happen to these people. They'll survive, that's what will happen. They've been surviving for generations like that. You and I might die before them. Come on, man. You should know them. They can live anywhere – and get fat, too. Live in a fowl-coop, a pig-sty if necessary. They can adjust to anything.

LANDOWNER: That's not totally true….

MERCHANT: Well, nothing is totally true. But you know what I mean. They'll live. You're not responsible for them.

LANDOWNER: Sometimes I wonder who is….I'll miss them in a strange way….They weren't really rude or anything….

MERCHANT: You hardly ever saw them. Anyway, we didn't come here to discuss that kind of thing. Business, that's the order of the day. When my factory goes up, and the shopping centre below it – you'll see. Best dam' thing that

ever happened to them. I mean, some of them will get work,
you know.

LANDOWNER: Yes, yes, that's true. Well....I think I'll speak to
the parson. He has a lot of influence with them and I'm sure
he can persuade them to leave without too much fuss and
bad feeling.

MERCHANT: Alright, do that! Now let's just conclude the whole
affair, if you don't mind. It's important that the factory is
completed by next April.

They produce documents, scan them intently. MERCHANT *signs.*
LANDOWNER *signs. They shake hands. Hands slapped. The 'music' for
the dance begins, a dry stacatto percussion. A grotesque dance-mime
develops. The* PASTOR *comes in. The three move spontaneously into this
weird dance-mime: John Crow.*
NARRATOR *comes on stage, obviously confused and annoyed.* JACK*'s voice
is heard off-stage, 'Hold on, man'.* NARRATOR *stops.* JACK *comes on.*

JACK: You noh answer me yet. How he could *own* the land? What
you mean by *owning*? A man cyah *own* land! He can take
care of it. And if he take care of it, it come to him like is his
sister and mother and him woman – if he love it. But how he
going *own* it? You have education; tell me.

NARRATOR: ...Well...he pay for it....

JACK: Money. (*taking out a coin*) How this could give him land?
(*flings it down between them*) Is just a piece of tin. If me have
the machine me could make it.

NARRATOR: You confusing me now....

JACK: I doan want confuse you. I only want know. (*almost
pleading*) If I doan know, I cyah sleep. If I even sleep, I wake
up.

NARRATOR: But look how much people doan know and dem not
in no worries to sleep.

JACK: Dem doan have to try sleep. Dem never wake up from the
day dem born.

NARRATOR: Cha man, Jack! Forget dem things there. Best you
just make your drum, play dem, sell dem...Live!

JACK (*waits silently, then...*): You doan answer me yet. How he
come to own the land?

NARRATOR (*shouting*): I doan know! He buy it, to shit! Jack man, you going on as though you doan understand. If the man say to move, we just have to move. I doan like it. But we have to move.

JACK: He own you then? You is him property?

NARRATOR: How you mean?

JACK: Why you moving?

NARRATOR: 'Cause if me noh move, police and soldier going run my ass out!

JACK: Oh! Is that then? Is through he have the law on his side? Suppose the law wrong?

NARRATOR: Jack, you know that doan matter. We have to move.

JACK: How come the law not on you side?

NARRATOR: Sake o' that same dam piece o'tin there. We noh have enough o' them piece o'tin.

JACK: And you noh going have enough, no time at all. The more you have, the more you going feel you have to have. And dem will always have more than you. Moffat noh have enough?

NARRATOR: Well…

JACK: Wha you want? You have to make up your mind wha you really want. Right now you want what Moffat have. I doan fight that. But right now you only going get it in the same way as him. You go have to turn oppressor. You go have to become Moffat. You go have to buy me and sell me. Have to say you *own* land, *own* building, even if you know is a lie.

NARRATOR: Jack, you know me noh have no intention—

JACK: No! you noh have no intention. But the intention there before you. Is that I find out. Once you start sing them song, you have to finish it. And dem want everyone sing dem song. Dem sing lead, you sing chorus. And all who singing chorus, dem ambition is to lead the singing one day. That is how dem keep the song going. You know how long this song singing? Four hundred years. White and Black sing it. White sing lead and Black sing chorus. But is one song. I does hear it the loudest in the city, night and day, but it everywhere.

NARRATOR: Jack—

JACK: Listen! I not singing that song. I beating my drum. My

voice different. If it sing that song, it will break. But listen,
you must know that song you going sing for the rest of your
living. (NARRATOR *tries to interrupt*) Listen! Change it or it
going change you — y'hear? Y'hear? And stop tell me
foolishness about Moffat own land. That is words. That is a
trick. He capture it with this (*picking up coin*) and with the
gun and bayonet hiding in this....No one own it, no one!

NARRATOR: We still have to move though.

JACK: Uh-huh! We still singing dem song. And that part of the
song say we must move — so we have to move. When we
start listen to the drum and drum say no slave and no
master, no landlord and tenant, no businessman and
labourer, no upper class and lower class, when we hear we
own drum (*touching his breast*) say that, we self going stop
that old song of oppression.

A single voice off-stage starts wailing out 'Hosanna, I build me house'.
Voices take it up. The villagers come on stage. A dance-mime of uprooting,
flight, weariness, essentially folk in style. Transition into the city, a
reggae rhythm, 'stills' and flashes of the urban ethos — 'dread' elements,
whores, city-slickers. Minor, but crucial, adjustments in costume — onstage
may be necessary. JACK *is the one person who doesn't join. He is looking*
on, troubled, as darkness falls on the whole scene.

Movement 2

JACK *is on-stage, unobtrusive, brooding. Two women enter, one clearly*
somewhat better off than the other, although they are undoubtedly both of
working-class origin

WOMAN 1: Me see Winston, this morning. So you know Winston
— noh suit you fi waste time wid him. So me say: 'Gimme a
money, nuh.' Hear him to me now 'That's all you all
woman want, eh?' Me have fi jes' laugh like sey is a big joke,
but it hurt me, you see. Him renk! Wha else me mus' want
from him? To how t'ings a go dem day dere, if you nah
defen' breads, you nah gwan wid a t'ing. Him better know
dat! That's why you see me stick wid de old man wey me

have dere. Da work dere a de shop was a kill me. An' all like how me have Rodney pickney fi dam' well mind – my friend dere is de right t'ing.

WOMAN 2: You know sey me noh really know him? How him stay? How old him is?

WOMAN 1: Lawd, me shame, me cyah tell you. Him nice though. Him love me! Treat me like gold. But through him sorta old, him cyah really...y'know? But him really nice. Ay! me hope sey dem two bredder dare soon reach on and noh have we a wait 'pon dem.

WOMAN 2: Dem soon come, man.

WOMAN 1: Dem better!...But how it go? A long time we noh really see one another fi chat. What go on dem day dere?

WOMAN 2: Still dere pon de road-work. Me nah get better dan dat fi now. And me lucky still fi get it, 'cause you know sey me nah really defend de politics t'eory. Is through de foreman, still. Him wan' try a t'ing, but him a watch me still.

WOMAN 1: Road-work. Me hear sey it have money. A true?

WOMAN 2: Have enough fi wha' you a do. 'Cause most time you noh do nuttin' – pick up two, three piece o' rubbish, then sit down. Me disgusted wid it.

WOMAN 1: But mus'! Somebody like you souldn' have fi waste time in dem dere foolishness. Me 'member you as a brainist. Spanish and all dem sinting dere. Mussy forgot all that now, eh?

WOMAN 2: Lawd me sis, you can eat Spanish? Spanish can buy something out a shop? Then nuh must forget it?

JACK (*who has been listening, interrupts suddenly*): Who in charge?

WOMAN 1: Jesus Christ!

JACK: Who in charge? I wan't know who run it. Is who?

WOMAN 1: Me say, de dam' idiot man mek me frighten!

JACK: Who control it?

WOMAN 2 (*intrigued*): Who control what?

WOMAN 1: Wha him a chat say?

JACK (*almost pleading*): Who rule? Who is de ruler of the city? Who beating the heart of the city?

WOMAN 1: But see here –

WOMAN 2 (*interested, though amused*): Wha' you wan' know dat for?

JACK: The ruler – I have to talk to him.

WOMAN 1: Eh-eh, but what a way you official. Better mind dem
    noh—

JACK: Where he is! Is him to stop it, not me. Where he is? Who
    he is?

WOMAN 1: Listen, doh mek no blasted noise wid me! A me is de
    mayor? (*to* WOMAN 2) Ain't is de mayor in charg o' de city?
    Or de prime minister? Me doh know how dem t'ing dere go.
    (WOMAN 2 *is silent*) Eh Audrey…a de mayor nuh?

WOMAN 2: A dat me a wonder…come to me like is not no man a
    rule de city…Something else…

WOMAN 1: A what den?

WOMAN 2: I doan know. But is it rule…rule de mayor, de prime
    minister, rule everybody.

Two men, FRANK *and* TONY, *come on in rhythm. One keeps up a
background chant, the other is doing a dee-jay dub ad lib.*

TONY (*chanting*): A-dunny, a-dunny, a-dunny, a-dunny…

FRANK: Who's got the dalski as I would say?
    Well I've got it and that means I've got you too,
    all along the way…yeah!
    Ooh Baby, if I didn't have it, what would I do? 'Cause I
    know, if I didn't have it, I wouldn't have you!
    A-dunny dunny dunny
    Dunny is the thing that make you kind.
    Put the power in your hand and make you rule the land.
    And it doan matter how you make it
    Anyhow it come, just take it…Huh!

*Break. Rocking footstomp timing by all. Then the women ease into the
chant.*

WOMEN: A-gimme, a-gimme, a-gimme, a-gimme…

FRANK: Uh-uh!
    You can't get it so easy.
    No you can't get it so easy.
    Cause-you-is-not-a-businessman-and-you-noh-have-no-
    land-and-you-is-not-a-politician-as-I-would-say.
    So you can't get it so easy.

WOMAN 1: A-gimme, a-gimme...   *refrain*
WOMAN 2: I gotta have it...
FRANK: Why you have fi have it?
WOMEN: [*Refrain*]
FRANK: I say, why you have fi have it?
WOMEN: [*Refrain*]
FRANK: See if you can do without it.
WOMEN: [*Refrain*]
FRANK: Hes' see if you can do without it.
WOMEN: [*Refrain*]
FRANK: Tek you hand out o' my pocket! Yeah!

They burst into laughter. FRANK *digs in his pocket, throws up coins and bills. Scramble, laughter. Just before they leave he throws a fifty-cent coin to* JACK. *They leave, rocking.* JACK *stares at the coin, picks it up.*

JACK (*looking at coin*): Garvey...Marcus Garvey. What you doing there? What you doing there! You shoulda here, right here, to help me before I get too tired. I start feel tired already. And I doan even start yet. What they put you there for? You cyah do nothing there! To mock we? To tell we dem could buy and sell we? Dem cyah do it! Cyah happen. Buy we labour, but cyah buy we. But is only that I so tired. Is that now. Tired. And I still doan know who to go to. The city...the monster eating it own children....I have to see the one, have to show him. Where my memory? It in my bag. Which part I put my bag? (*looking around*)...I keeping all we memory together in the bag, because everyone forgetting. (*picks up the bag, looks at the coin in his hand*) But what dem put you dere for?...I have to see the ruler....

JACK *goes off quickly, urgently. The* NARRATOR *comes on from the other side of the stage.*

NARRATOR: Of course, he never got to speak to no ruler. He try to see the mayor, is what I hear, and never even reach as far as the mayor secretary. And he lucky still, he could o' end up in prison. Because police stop him from outside, asking him all kinda question – what he have in the bag, what's his

intention but he answering as how he see it and the police
decide he mussy not too righted. Dem let him go. It make
him realize that no way he oulda ever get to speak with any
ruler. Thing is, he never fully understand at the time that is
not no man he have to look for in no special office. But still,
after that, he stop ask people question. He asking the city
itself. He look pon on all the buying and selling, the crowd
on the sidewalk wha' never stop moving, car on the street
up and down, all day long, whore-dem selling themself a
night-time, christian wailing in church 'bout their sorrows.
Looking 'pon everything, him meditate himself into almost
madness. He was starting to get 'fraid of him round that
time and sorta feel-a way shame too. One time me see him
and hide, 'cause…and him used to make me dizzy wid him
talk. See too much. And what him see start to make a
strange kinda sense.

City noises become audible towards the end of the NARRATOR's *speech.
The city sprawls on stage – market people, business people, shoppers in
mannequin positions, newspaper vendors, whores. The sound of a fife or
mouth-organ wailing a hymn is heard right through. People snap in and
out of roles, movement slows, speeds up, paces normally, freezes. The whole
crazy melange sorts itself out into a church meeting; the* PASTOR *prepares
to address his flock.*

PASTOR: Greetings, brother, sister, friend, in the name of our
Lord and ruler. He is our answer tonight, amen? (*loud chorus
of 'Amen'*) He is the answer to all our problems, alleluia!
(*chorus of 'that's right, 'preach it', etc.*) So let us first make a
joyful noise unto the ruler of our lives. Turn to page 50, song
number 44.

A bizarre 'song of silence'. Everyone is obviously straining to sing, the
PASTOR *leading vigorously. There is not a sound. The 'song' ends.*

PASTOR: Amen! What a beautiful thing it is when we know we
have meaning in our lives and can sing of that meaning. O,
how wonderful! (*chorus of voices*) And now we will ask
Brother Hughes to lead us in prayer.

HUGHES *stands and prepares to address them. A burst of applause is the signal for the transmutation into a businessman's convention.*

HUGHES: Thank you, thank you. Fellow colleagues, aspirants in our business world, partners in my firm, ladies and gentlemen. I may as well come straight to the point. I do not like to – I assure you it is not my usual method of approach – but the situation is serious and demands it. We are approaching something like a crisis. The very basis of our system of free enterprise has been challenged – and I will not say successfully – but it has been challenged. We cannot ignore it. This challenge must be met!

Burst of applause that gradually, smoothly changes into a rhythmic hand-clap, the last verse of a 'song'. The PASTOR *again brings this 'song' to a close and continues.*

PASTOR: And the kingdom of heaven is likened unto…'

What follows is a reading of Matthew ch. 25, v. 14–18. There is a burst of applause from the congregation.

PASTOR: Brother Hughes.
HUGHES: It would be dangerous to bury our heads in the sand now and hope that our house will stand firm. No! We must tighten our ranks and try – by all means possible – to eliminate these threats to the principles of free enterprise, regardless of what level of society they originate from. There can be no compromise, in the final analysis. If a policy is gnawing at the very root of our system, that policy must go. In this battle there can be only one victor, one ruler.

Briefly, flatly, chorus of 'I shall not be moved'.

PASTOR: And after a long time…

He continues reading Matthew ch. 25, v. 19–29. There is a burst of applause and then the other speaker chimes in.

HUGHES: Those who complain of the injustices of capitalism
must realize that all are not born equal. All cannot be
expected to live equally. Why must we leave an
air-conditioned existence to sweat in a hot poverty that
everyone is running from? We worked – according to our
principles – for what we have. We used our talents. I hear
that some of our businessmen are becoming almost
ashamed of being businessmen, because of these new,
pernicious ideas among us. I say, if you can multiply a
hundredfold, then by all means do so. What would happen
to the Red Cross and Salvation Army and other charitable
institutions without our contributions? (*applause*)
Colleagues, I urge you to use your God-given talents to help
create prosperity in the nation. If sometimes we seem not to
care for the lower levels of the society, they must remember
that we, too, have our problems and charity, after all,
begins at home. Finally, let me repeat, we must spare no
effort to help eliminate this virus and bring things back to
what they were before.

*Burst of applause that goes into the rhythm of the 'victim dance'. The
dancers move out, converge on* JACK *who has been standing apart, looking
on.*

CHORUS: Buy something
Sell something
Do anything to make a living
Beg you ten cent
You doh pay rent! Buh wha! you a say?
You noh eat for today?
Sell de dam' drum.
G'way
Let us pray.
Buy something
Sell something
Keep the system going.

Convergence. JACK *screams, lost among them. Darkness. In the darkness,
the Drum-maker's song.*

(*Chorus*)
    Long time now
    I-Man looking but couldn't see
    Now I see
    I find myself facing history
    All I see—
    Ignorance, pain and poverty
    But I cyah go back
    Forward now, what will be will be

1. Long time I hear this drum
    And it giving out one different sound
    And it tell me come.
    So I go
    Trying to know
    Where I from
    But business-man ruling me
    Preacher-man fooling me
    Police and soldier pursuing me to misery.

Chorus again, then Verse 2.

2. If I had my way
    I would break out of this net that bind me
    Try to run away
    But there's no
    where to go
    I must stay
    Still inside my own eyes now
    Where there are no lies now
    Although you won't hear whatever I try to say.

Chorus.

Movement 3

The NARRATOR *enters. There is a flute or mouth-organ playing off-stage.*

NARRATOR: Every evening the city slides out of its skin like an
    old hag, turns its insides out, spilling its bowels open. And

the stink rises. All in the gutters, all on the edges of the asphalt and the concrete sidewalks, garbage huddle itself together like a hunchback. All in the gutters, a kind of sick fluid start to run, fish-belly and old tripe and the blood of beasts slaughtered to keep man alive. All that…the orange peel, twist-up and dry, like old skin, mango seed, old bananas, yellow and black and dead. Round in the evening is when you start to see what the city is all about. The fruit of all man-work here is stinking garbage. During the day, in the sun-hot, city eating out man and woman labour: woman in store selling things and more things and more and more things, man stretch out under car and truck belly, salesman hustling from nowhere to nowhere, secretary clack-clack-clack on the typewriter, is like the sound of her life hurrying away on high heels. That is the city all day, that is what it eating. In the evening, it piss it out into the gutters, shit it on the streets and sidewalks. No matter how much of man and woman substance it eat, in the evening, all come down. Garbage is the fruit and the chief produce of the city. The ruler never satisfy. Tomorrow he will want another sacrifice of labour. But who is this ruler? Same question turn Jack around, turn his eyes inside. No one ever see no ruler. But they see his temples everywhere; The Covenant of Barclay, The Royal Temple, First Temple of Chicago…not too long ago, there was a crusade to bring in the worshippers who couldn't worship at the bigger temples. They start a smaller church called The Workers Salvation Temple. But who is this ruler? Right now, if you ask Jack – and if he answer you – he will say something about a snake. Or serpent. At least that is how he show it to me before he…well, that is how he feel it the last time he ever speak to me.

Music continues as NARRATOR *fades into falling darkness, music. The light comes back to reveal* JACK *and* NARRATOR.

JACK (*calm*): I does see now, you know. I see things. You know it
have a serpent now coil all around us, right as we talking
here? You doan know that. And same time, we inside the
serpent belly? You doan know that. And it body stretch
around many several different place, country I doan even
know about, but it there. It want to wrap itself round the
whole world.

NARRATOR: Jack, what you saying?

JACK (*earnest*): The serpent! Is it Sssssss…it coil itself round and
squeezing out all your life and labour and…everything, and
it talking soft all the while…Sssssss…

NARRATOR (*suspicious*): Jack, what happen?

JACK: Lies. You know is lies keeping it alive. And labour.
Everyone working hard to keep it alive. They believe if it die
they will die too. Even who know better still cyah do
better…Lies, and labour…Sssssss…

NARRATOR: Jack…I mean, what you doing? I mean…alright!
why you doan kill this snake you seeing?

JACK: I is just a warning. I is nothing else. If you see you see. If
you doan see…I is still a warning.

NARRATOR: Alright, so you's a warning! But you doan have to go
round the place like, like a…madman! Collecting rubbish
in your bag! What difference that making?

JACK: You know what I have in there? (*horrified*)

NARRATOR: What?

JACK (*emptying the garbage*): That is the history of my people! I
making a voice now, with that, for people to hear, because
they cyah see. I making a voice with anything. Because
everything have to speak for we or everything will speak
against we. The same piece of wood, old chain, oil drum,
piece of iron – if we doan make them talk for us of who we is,
what happening to us, they will tell the whole world a
different history…of shame. That is why I did start make
drum. Drum is the heart-voice and the memory of freedom.
(*holding his hand against his heart*) When your brain forget, the
drum remember. Everybody jus want sleep, but even when
you sleeping, your heart still beating, your memory noh
stop. That is why I did make drum. Drum is the

heart-voice, the memory of freedom. I collecting these things to make drum.

NARRATOR (*convinced that* JACK *is on the edge, but…*): But what use the drum remember? You tell me about a serpent. Drum will kill it?

JACK (*something breaks in him now, but also hardens his mind*): You doan even understand. And look how long I talking to you. The serpent inside you too. Is it eyes you seeing me with now. Is it tongue you talking with now. You doan see? You have to kill all the lies it saying in your head. You remember you tell me Moffat *own* land? You have to kill that. But is the drum, is only the memory of freedom will kill them lies. And you doan even understand. Oh God, I think you would understand. Anyway, I going.

NARRATOR: Where you going, Jack? It doan have nowhere to go.

JACK: I going.

NARRATOR: Where? (*he knows, deep down, what is happening*)

JACK: I tired, you see, I was really tired, y'know (*childlike, relieved*)

NARRATOR: Where!

JACK: I going….

He shoulders the bag and leaves. The sound of drums describe what happens to him. Darkness. NARRATOR *reappears.*

NARRATOR: I doan know…when a man see, and he doan know what to do about what he seeing…well…what? I suppose he must choose…. (*brooding, as a flurry of people come rushing to catch the last bus; he watches them*)…the last bus, (*he starts to move off, stops*) same old road, going the same place…. (*stops, shakes his head*) Uh-uh. (*walks off the other way.*)

CURTAIN

Textual notes

The language of the play

The author makes the following comment on the original script:

Apologies must be made for a somewhat awkward switch in
styles of speech, evident on the page, specifically in the case of
the Narrator and Jack. The presentation was written with
actual people in mind for these roles and as it became apparent
that there might be need for a switch, the speech accordingly
shifted. Till a reworking of the script, actors in these roles must
feel free to mould the speech patterns into a more unified
whole, provided no difference in meaning is added or sub-
tracted.

Actors who belong to the theatre groups that attempted the
play have found the author's fears not really well founded, as
they have been able to adopt fairly easily to the shift in speech
patterns. It is interesting, though, that Mr Hippolyte should
make this suggestion, as it helps to point us to those rhythms
and cadences which make an individual's speech truly individual.

Another point that the reader may wish to consider is that the
playwright is a St Lucian but the play was written while he was
living and teaching in Jamaica and was set in Jamaica and
intended for a Jamaican cast.

On another note, some changes in the text may be made to
accommodate the wishes of some school administrators who
would prefer strong language to be excluded from any play with
which their youngsters are associated. On pages 131 and 135 'to
shit' can be eliminated; 'shut-your-ass' (page 131) can changed
to 'shut your mouth'; run my ass' (page 135) to 'run me';
'whore-dem' (page 140) to 'prostitutes-dem'.

Detailed notes

page
127   Beg you two shilling: May I have two shillings please? I
       beg of you.

doan: don't.

why you put his face on the fifty cent?: the face of Marcus
Garvey is on the Jamaica 50c coin.

128 mussy: must be.

him no old to that: he is not that old.

when you check it: when you think about it.

cyah: can't.

129 pickney: child/children.

131 as decent somebody: like decent people.

131 You let dem fool you, make you say such a thing: You have
let them fool you into saying such a thing.

132 facety: fiesty.

134 cha man!: come on man!

135 Is through he have: Is it because he has

Sake o': because of.

I doan fight that: I am not opposing or condemning you for
that.

136 noh suit you fi: It wouldn't be to your advantage to.

gimme a money, nuh: give me some money (a coin, a note)
please.

me have fi jes' laugh like sey is: I simply have to laugh as if
it is.

renk: fiesty, offensive in behaviour (used contemptuously).

to how t'ings a go dem day here: in the light of what's
happening these days.

defen' breads: have money as one's main focus.

yuh nah gwan wid a t'ing: you're not making a serious
effort to better yourself.

137 An' all like how me have Rodney pickney fi...mind: When
one considers that I also have Rodney's child to rear.

How him stay?: what does he look like?

me hope sey dem two bredder dare soon reach on: I hope
that those two 'brothers' soon arrive.

a wait 'pon dem: waiting for them.

fi chat: to have a conversation, to talk.

mi lucky still fi get it: Anyhow I am lucky to have got it.

mi nah defend de politics t'eory: I am not interested in
politics.

him wan' try a t'ing, but him a watch me still: he is
interested in starting a relationship, but at the moment he
is only watching me.

brainist: 'bright', clever, student.

dem sinting dere: things like that.

then nuh must forget it?: then oughtn't I to (and is it not inevitable that I would) forget it?

wha him a chat say?: what is he saying?

138 Better mind dem noh…: Be careful that they don't…

a dee-jay dub: a kind of 'rapping' done to reggae beat that was popularized in Jamaica by Hugh Roy and other disc jockeys, and later by yet others like King Yellowman.

dunny: money (combination of 'done' meaning 'finished' and 'money').

dalski: dollars.

139 you shoulda here: you should be here.

140 no way he oulda ever get: there is no way that he could get.

145 I does see now: I see now. (This construction is not a Jamaican creole one and is an example of Mr Hippolyte's St Lucian (English based) creole creeping into the speech of his characters.)

146 Is it eyes you seeing me with: You are seeing me through its eyes.

It doan have nowhere to go: There is nowhere (for you) to go.

Questions for the class or cast

1. (*page* 129) Why does the drum crescendo and then die to a 'raging stammer'? What is the significance of this?
2. (*page* 129) What does Jack mean when he says that the drums must make everyone hear? And see? See what? How?
3. (*page* 130) How does the boy respond to the opportunity/ excuse to play the drum? Does this have any significance (in light of what happens later)?
4. (*page* 130) What kind of rhythm does the boy play? How does this rhythm differ from that which Jack plays?
5. (*pages* 131–2) What are the dreams which are bursting to come out of the drum?
6. (*page* 132) What is the significance of the reference to Moffat at the end of the argument about 'power'?
7. (*page* 133) Is Moffat the person with the power? How does he differ from the Merchant?
8. (*page* 134) What does this dance 'say' about the Pastor?

9. (*page* 134) Why does Jack believe that the Narrator must now 'know'?

10. (*page* 137) Is the second Woman's comment on her Spanish an implied criticism of the education system? Or on the social system?

11. (*page* 137) In what way does Jack's question underline the discussion between the two women?

12. (*page* 139) Is the reference to a 'bag of memories' a weak one? Or does it work here?

13. (*page* 140) 'Thing is…is not no man he have to look for in no special office.' Does this mean that the Narrator now knows who is 'in charge'? What are the implications (whether he does or not) of this for his relationship with Jack?

14. (*page* 139) Why did the Narrator hide when he saw Jack?

15. (*pages* 142–3) What is Jack's reaction to the chant which surrounds him – with an almost overwhelming insistence – that he abandon his idea of how life should be lived?

16. (*page* 145) The Narrator, who since he was young has known Jack, refers to the contents of his bag as 'rubbish'. What does this tell us about him at this point? What would Jack's reaction be?

17. (*page* 146) What happens to Jack at the end? What do the drums tell us?

18. (*page* 146) What is the significance/meaning of the serpent image? Why has the author chosen a snake as the image to use?

19. (*page* 129) What does the drum symbolize?

20. (*pages* 145-6) How can the drum battle the serpent?

21. (*pages* 134–6) What is the basis of Jack's argument on 'owning the land' and of his making a connection between this and owning people?

22. (*page* 135) What are the implications of Jack's assertion that the law can be wrong? Is the law wrong? Is the law wrong for being 'on Moffat's side'? What are the reverberations of all of this?

23. (*pages* 135–6) What is Jack's implied solution to the problem of power relationships in the society?

24. (*page* 143) How important is Jack's song to the message of the play?

25. (*page* 129) The Narrator and the Boy are the same person. Can one actor play the two parts and be convincing? If so, what would he have to do (with his body, voice, and so on) to ensure this? If not, how can two actors be presented, to suggest that they represent one person at different stages of life?

26. (*page* 131) Is the line 'you doan have no power Jack' a very important one? If you think it is, how would you, if you were the actors, underline, or 'punch' it?

27. (*page* 132) 'Of course, me never ask no one a dam' thing.' Is this a humorous line? If so, what does it tell us about the Narrator? If not, how should it be played to ensure that no one sees it as funny?

28. (*page* 133) When the Merchant says 'They can live anywhere', is his tone matter-of-fact or sneering? What is the implication of each of these interpretations?

29. (*page* 137) 'Who in charge?' What is Jack's demeanour when he starts to speak? What is it that draws the kind of reaction he gets?

30. (*pages* 137–8) (a) What is it about Jack that intrigues the second Woman enough for her to engage him in conversation? If Jack looked and sounded like an ordinary madman or indigent, would she have? (b) What is it about her that makes her pause long enough to realize that there is something in what Jack is saying?

Production notes

The style of the play

This is documentary theatre. By nature, this type of drama lends itself to group experimentation, improvisation work and so on.

The writer calls at times for dance/mime sequences. These can't simply crop up. It implies a whole style for the play: a lot of stylization, maybe, choreographed crowd scenes, or anything that would create a style into which these scenes could fit easily.

Again these dances *must carry the play forward*. There must be a difference in the quality of the dance mime on page 136 to the earlier one on page 134, to show that there have been some changes in the quality of the lives of the people – changes which they have internalized.

A teacher should not let this faze him. The easy answer, that of asking a dance teacher to choreograph these moments, may produce less effective and, to the youngsters, less exciting work than if the group did it themselves. One way is for the group to 'work out' in mime, all the moments when dance mime is needed, then stylize the mime, then extend parts of it to dance. At this point a dance teacher can come in to assist in cleaning it up. (Unless, of course, a dance teacher is involved in the work from the outset.)

Set design

This *must* be flexible. A couple of platforms of different shapes and sizes (one high enough to become in turn a table, a desk and a small raised dais) are all that is needed as set. Some productions have added a serpent (lowered from the fly tower at the end of the play), bent in the shape of an S or more correctly a dollar sign ($: an S bent around a stick).

Everything is created by the bodies of the actors. Changes in place, time and persons are made effective by the body language, groupings, and so on.

Lighting

If you have fairly good lighting facilities available you can experiment with the effects of various colour combinations and levels of illumination. It may be advisable not to use too many effects, though, as the play is already full of symbols and images. Lighting can be used to indicate the passage of time, flashbacks and the like. It can also help to underline the effect of the dance-mime. The danger lies in the attempt to use colours, and so on, to create mood. If they are overused the action of the play may seem unreal and the play lose its immediacy. It can also lead the audience to see symbols and deeper meanings which you did not intend and do not wish to imply.

Costumes

Simple, everyday costumes can be used. The more elaborate these are the more limiting. It is inadvisable to have any pauses in the action for costume changes. So the less the costumes limit the actors to any time, place or occasion, the better. The Landowner, Merchant and Pastor can use simple additions to a basic costume (a jacket, a collar) to help establish their characters.

One should also be careful to avoid making Jack look simply like a 'bag-and-pan' madman. You may wish to differentiate him from these by having him appear clean always or by using some such device.

Some points to consider

The songs

Melodies may be composed or borrowed. Authentic folk melodies should be used for folk material.

The drum

Drumming is important in the play. The drum (sound) is an important 'character' and director and cast could find it a quite interesting exercise to search for ways in which this can be underlined.

Transitions

Some of these are difficult:

(a) On page 143 the writer calls for the drum-maker's song to be sung in the darkness after the chant (by the chorus) ends. It is a long time to ask the audience to sit in the dark and some groups may wish to do something with it. One suggestion is that, in very dim light, there is some sort of dance-sequence on stage. Another is that for some of the time we see Jack on a raised platform singing the song, playing his drum softly.

(b) Page 144, second transition: if the character of the

Narrator has been developing all along – or if he is played as an omniscient presence, the transition to this poetic unfolding of one of the main themes of the play can be made fairly easily.

(c) The transition on pages 144–5 may be a bit jarring but if one experiments a bit it can jar in a positive way – bringing the reverie of the Narrator down to the practical 'earth' of Jack's philosophy.

(d) The change on page 141 between the church (middle-and working-class) and the (upper middle-class) businessman's convention, is an interesting actor's exercise. The body language, demeanour, rhythm, and so on, change tremendously each time the shift is made.

Important moments

Page 127: Jack's voice, coming out of the darkness, should be sharp, startling, clear.

Page 132: 'Is who in charge?' The theme of power reverberates through the play. Whenever it surfaces the players should be aware. Note, for example, the significance of making reference to Mr Moffat at the end of the discussion on power.

Page 136: The two women are meant to represent 'types' in the society. This could be reflected in their physical appearance, body language and so on, as well as in their attitudes.

Pages 136–8: One needs to consider why scenes like this are included. Is it to: (a) show an aspect of the life of the people? (b) show the passage of time? (c) document Jack's deterioration? As a bit of documentary theatre the full purpose of these scenes should be internalized in order for the play to work as a whole.

Page 138: The timing of the 'a-dunny' moment is vital. One may choose to make it not *too* obviously an answer to the question on page 138, but to have it appear almost coincidental.

Page 138: The movement here ought to tie in with the dance-mime technique that marks the style of the play as a whole.

Page 139: An actor should consider, very carefully, the effect on the audience of his playing of Jack's reaction to seeing Garvey's face on the 50c coin. Does the author want a laugh?

Page 132: This is the first moment since page 128 that the Narrator comes on to speak directly to the audience. One should be careful to prevent it jarring. If no stylized/ritualized method which can fit into the general style of the play can be evolved, one may have to find a way to make the changes like this more fluent. One can, for example, make the Narrator enter earlier and observe Jack; or use a Narrator who never leaves the stage.

5 The improvised play

When we use the word 'improvisation' here we will be using it in one particular sense – to describe a method of moulding a dramatic sequence out of the participants' own creativity while they are under the guidance of a teacher/director. In this sense the improvised play is, strictly speaking, created by the group. The process can begin and/or end with one person (a teacher/director or anyone else), but the whole group helps to decide on such things as the dialogue, aspects of the plot, and relationships between characters.

Why improvise?

The teacher may have one or more reasons for choosing this method of working.

(a) He may, as an individual, have something that he wishes to say to the school (or general) audience, which he thinks can be expressed more powerfully if he works with his youngsters in its creation. There can also be some issue, some theme, with which the teacher wishes to deal and on which no suitable scripted play can be found.

(b) He may realize that his student-actors have something that they urgently wish to say and so may choose this medium as one which is suitable for the expression of this idea/desire/grievance.

(c) He may simply find that none of the scripted plays he can lay his hands upon excite the group and so he may decide that they should do their own.

(d) The drama club in the school may have evolved to the stage where they wish to experiment with something other than scripted plays.

(e) The most important reason is probably that many teachers use the creating of a play by a group of youngsters as an educative exercise. The treatment by the group, in this creative way, of a moral or ethical issue, can have a truly ennobling and fulfilling effect. Teachers, therefore, often opt for this type of

drama as a result of their recognition of the educational value of
the exercise.

Some advantages

In improvisational work the *group* is the key factor. All persons
need to respect it and give in to it. The team-spirit demanded, in
an atmosphere of achievement and fun, can develop the social
skills of its members. The teacher/director can encourage the
actors to support each other and to truly share the creative
experience. They begin to realize then that 'scene-stealing' in
this type of work is worse than larceny and to appreciate the
fragility of a work during its creation. The type of play which is
most likely to succeed when one uses this approach is one
without obvious 'stars' – even though some roles may eventually be bigger than others. During its creation, the development of
the total play dictates the development of the roles in it and
students learn to turn their energies to all the parts that make up
the whole.

Prerequisites

Eagerness – the people involved must feel some level of
excitement about using this technique. This may result from the
fact that the students are having a chance to say something to
the world, or the teacher has come up with an exciting theme, or
the group eagerly wishes to try this method. If, on the other
hand, the students really wish to be given a script to learn their
lines and work in the traditional way, they should be allowed to
do so – unless the teacher is positive that he can fire them with
his own enthusiasm for this approach.

   Time – there must be enought time allotted to toss around
ideas, experiment with approaches, create a play and then hone
it into a good performance piece. Although the principle that
'pressure makes diamonds' is generally true, the whole process
may prove of little real value if the play is thrown together in a
couple of weeks just to satisfy some requirement. There are of
course exceptions to this: a group of high school students in

Kingston once improvised a play in a hurry because the school principal refused to allow them to go ahead with the play they had been rehearsing for the Schools Drama Festival. They created their own play around the incidents that led to the refusal and their reactions to it! The principal was a fine enough educator to allow this one to be performed – even though it was critical of the school administration. The play worked very well.

Bravery – it is no good attempting this type of production if the teacher/director is unwilling to experiment or to try out ideas that may seem at the outset 'wild' or confused. Students, when motivated, can, if they feel that it will be taken seriously, make the most outrageous suggestions. Occasionally these will be brilliant, extremely creative and exciting.

Approaching the improvisation

Ten points to remember

1. *Avoid verbosity or overstatement.* Drama is *action* and it is the visual that is often most important. Moreover, when the dialogue in a play is pruned to its barest bones, what is left is often more poignant and more powerful than was originally there.

2. *Use bodies.* Grouping, body language, body rhythms, can help to make statements and to deepen the meaning of a play. So, in creating a play it is often helpful to constantly think of ways in which the use of the actors' physical presence on stage can help to bring across your total message.

3. *Avoid the temptation to ultra-realism.* Improvisation should never deal entirely with realistic scenes from everyday life. The material must be visualized through theatrical eyes. Make sure that the story or idea is expressed in terms of the theatre, using theatrical conventions and obeying theatrical rules.

Realism which is based on the photographic representation of actual everyday life may limit too strictly the stage representation of certain subjects.

4. *Concentrate on developing interesting situations.* When this is done, character development and interpersonal relationships will develop almost automatically as a result. At the same time,

a play with interesting people in a dull or badly conceived situation is far less entertaining than a play with sketchily drawn characters in an interesting situation.

5. *Avoid 'tyranny'*. Giving the youngsters some freedom to experiment helps them to develop as persons, while at the same time it includes their own creativity in the playmaking process – which will most often result in a better play. Sometimes, very early in the process, a teacher may already have a storyline in his or her mind. The temptation not to allow any amendments to it should be avoided as it may negate some of the positive effects of the whole exercise.

6. *Avoid over-indulgence*. This is as serious an offence as 'tyranny'. The teacher should always be there to guide and to act as an arbiter.

7. *Inspire always*. Be encouraging and try to create a positive atmosphere always. In rehearsal, when energy drags, or when the work seems to be pure drudgery, stop the session.

8. *Arrive at a final script*. It is probably safer to do this than to carry the purely improvisational approach up to the actual performance. Inexperienced performers are often unpredictable when playing to an actual audience.

9. *Be flexible*. Avoid having a tight rehearsal schedule where you set yourself difficult progress targets. Simply try to achieve as much as possible each time. When the final script is arrived at and cleaning up is being done, you can plan more tightly.

10. *Work for clarity*. Avoid confusing the audience by trying to cram too much material into the script. During early rehearsals, all ideas can be discussed and new ways of plot-development can be tried out, but eventually all must be sifted and the final product made into a coherent whole. You may even find that some of the better ideas that had to be left out may be a good jumping-off point for another play.

Some hints on procedure

Finding the base

Sometimes the group knows quite clearly what theme it wants to portray or experiment with. Occasionally the skeleton of the plot has been drafted before work begins. There are times, though, when the group knows only vaguely which theme it would like to treat, or there are times when it is the idea of improvisation *per se* that fascinates them, and so they are open to suggestions for ideas or topics on which to base their plot. In such a case discussions of matters of individual, group or societal interest may reveal a common concern which could lead to a plot idea or at least to a general theme.

There is also the more concrete stimulus. The lyrics of popular songs, newspaper reports, magazine articles or news items can provide this. Improvised plays have come in recent years from popular songs like 'Up Park Camp' (composed by Jacob Miller), 'Johnny Too Bad' (adapted by Bunny Wailer), 'No Vacancy' (Sugar Minott), 'I'm Born Again' (Boney M); and folk songs like 'Linstead Market' (Ja), 'Buddy Lindo' (Tobago) and 'Come Back Liza' (Ja).

Developing the plot

Here are a few brief notes on some of the things to bear in mind.
Keep it moving. In theatre boredom is unforgivable.
Keep it uncluttered. An audience is generally only capable of reacting to one thing at a time.
Keep it interesting – by variation: contrasts in moods, rhythms, pacing and characters should help to do this.
Use your actors' creativity. Move for spontaneity, not invention. Let them trust their instincts and avoid cleverness, cheap melodrama and cheap farce.
Avoid too much dialogue. It must express the scene's mood and/or the characters', but *no more*. Don't make any extraneous point while the action waits on you.
Start and end with a bang. Avoid long explanatory opening scenes. Capture audience interest and actor enthusiasm at the beginning of the play and avoid allowing the play to fizzle out. Students often enjoy this challenge and can be highly self-critical in exercises like this, so you can push them there.

Helping the actors

(a) Encourage 'total' acting: that is, immersion in character and

situation. The actors should be encouraged to continually
evaluate their own performances.

(b) Gently 'side-coach' them. You can get the students to
develop the ability to respond to a spoken stimulus (one or two
words) from you without stopping the action. This is important
during early rehearsals, as you would not want to stop a creative
moment to correct technical flaws while, on the other hand, you
may not wish to ignore something that can be improved upon
with a suggestion from you.

(c) Allow them to search for and develop their characters.
Discourage 'performing' in early sessions. When improvising a
play with too tight a deadline in mind you run the risk of
retarding the students' growth (as actors and as persons).
Never kill spontaneity – even if the spontaneous outburst
carries the plot in a direction which you consider tangential or
even undesirable.

(d) The cliché characters, e.g. 'old woman with walking stick'
or 'shifty-eyed villain' can often be valid, and work well, if group
experiments are allowed to reveal interesting variations of the
character.

(e) Attitudes, e.g. 'nobody loves me', 'the world owes me a
living', can be physicalized – these are good for experimentation.

(f) Animal characters can be used. They too can be physicalized. Or, on the other hand, animal characteristics given to
humans can be expressed by using the animal's physical
attributes.

Design

Suggestion in design is generally better than attempts at
realism. If your actors have created the play and have
internalized it, both as a group and individually, the parapher-
nalia of elaborate sets and costumes are not only unnecessary
but can be distracting or obstructive. They are also often quite
expensive.

An example of the evolution of an improvised play

The background

Some years ago I taught drama at a high school in Kingston,

Jamaica. The drama club at this school had been doing well in the schools' festival and national festival for some years. A tightly knit, well-disciplined group had emerged. Many of the students in the group who were to leave school that year wanted to do something extra, to go a step further – their own play.

One of them, Seymour, came with an outline for a play. The group was not happy with it but encouraged him as they knew he had talent as a writer.

At that same time another student, Winston, had had his first pop record released, a song called 'Sandra' which told the story of a boy who only realized how much he loved a girl after she had died. The idea came to many pesons at the same time: 'Let's base our play on Winston's song.'

Discussion centred around the way we ought to use the song and the group decided that it would mark the culmination of the action of the play, rather than the beginning. This gave us a limitation which we were lucky to be able to use to our advantage – the plot was not 'open' any more. The girl had to die.

The plot came slowly. Situations were experimented with; some led nowhere and were discarded, some helped us to create character and role relationships. Those scenes relating to the lives of the characters which were not used in the final script were still helpful in creating the feeling of rounded, real persons.

Developing the plot – using conflict

The questions which worked well were: what does she/he want? Always, the scenes which helped carry the play forward were those in which the conflicts between the characters were heightened, deepened, or broadened by the situations in which they found themselves.

Sometimes new characters had to be created in order to move the play forward. Occasionally completed scenes were partly redone in order to accommodate new developments later in the play.

Style

During improvisations (in the early stages) the suggestion was made and accepted that dances and songs would work in helping to move the play forward. This was, I think, partly because some members of the cast were ardent members of the school's dance club and were fascinated by the power of this medium. So the play became a musical. Two (short) scenes were done almost completely as dance/mime and this eventually affected the whole style of the play.

It may have been luck, but the plot worked itself out without the group having to force it at the end. It ended melodramatically but effectively. Directing this play was easy. The group did most of the work. I concentrated on giving it a style, a flow, and worked on getting things like the pacing right. The crew, who had been in on it from the start – co-operating with the actors on the very simple sets (which were designed by the group) – helped to get the play flowing slickly.

What we found was that even though two of the students showed extraordinary talent (one is now a professional dramatist), there were no 'stars' in the production. It belonged to everyone. In the final scripting of the plot all the outstanding decisions on details were left to Seymour. Yet all the students had a kind of proprietary interest in it.

The friendships that were formed among the students during this play were lasting. The growth that occurred in them was almost physically visible. As a teacher I probably *educated* more in these ten weeks than during the whole year in the classroom. I also grew tremendously as a teacher.

P.S. *Sandra* was entered in the Jamaica Festival Amateur Drama Competition. It won the following awards: Best Play, Best Director, Best Musical, Best Tragedy, Best Original Script, Best Actor, Best Actress; special awards for choreography, music and ensemble work as well as several other individual acting awards.